JUMP-STARTING
THE STALLED
FUNDRAISING
CAMPAIGN

W9-CLN-984

JUMP-STARTING THE STALLED FUNDRAISING CAMPAIGN

Julia Ingraham Walker

WILEY

John Wiley & Sons, Inc.

Published by John Wiley & Sons, Inc., Hoboken, New Jersey.
Published simultaneously in Canada.

For general information on our other products and services, or technical support, please contact our Customer Care Department within the United States at 800-762-2974, outside the United States at 317-572-3993 or fax 317-572-4002.

Wiley also publishes its books in a variety of electronic formats. Some content that appears in print may not be available in electronic books.

For more information about Wiley products, visit our Web site at http://www.wiley.com.

Library of Congress Cataloging-in-Publication Data:

ISBN-13: 978-0-470-49655-8

Printed in the United States of America

10 9 8 7 6 5 4 3 2 1

The AFP Fund Development Series

The AFP Fund Development Series is intended to provide fund development professionals and volunteers, including board members (and others interested in the nonprofit sector), with top-quality publications that help advance philanthropy as voluntary action for the public good. Our goal is to provide practical, timely guidance and information on fundraising, charitable giving, and related subjects. The Association of Fundraising Professionals (AFP) and Wiley each bring to this innovative collaboration unique and important resources that result in a whole greater than the sum of its parts. For information on other books in the series, please visit:

www.afpnet.org

The Association of Fundraising Professionals

The Association of Fundraising Professionals (AFP) represents over 30,000 members in more than 197 chapters throughout the United States, Canada,

Mexico, and China, working to advance philanthropy through advocacy, research, education, and certification programs.

The association fosters development and growth of fundraising professionals and promotes high ethical standards in the fundraising profession. For more information or to join the world's largest association of fundraising professionals, visit www.afpnet.org.

2008–2009 AFP Publishing Advisory Committee

Chair: Nina P. Berkheiser, CFRE
Principal Consultant, Your Nonprofit Advisor

Linda L. Chew, CFRE
Development Consultant

D. C. Dreger, ACFRE
Senior Campaign Director, Custom Development Solutions, Inc. (CDS)

Patricia L. Eldred, CFRE
Director of Development, Independent Living, Inc.

Samuel N. Gough, CFRE
Principal, The AFRAM Group

Audrey P. Kintzi, ACFRE
Director of Development, Courage Center

Steven Miller, CFRE
Director of Development and Membership, Bread for the World

Robert J. Mueller, CFRE
Vice President, Hospice Foundation of Louisville

Maria Elena Noriega
Director, Noriega Malo & Associates

Michele Pearce
Director of Development, Consumer Credit Counseling
  Service of Greater Atlanta

Leslie E. Weir, MA, ACFRE

Director of Family Philanthropy, The Winnipeg Foundation

Sharon R. Will, CFRE

Director of Development, South Wind Hospice

John Wiley & Sons, Inc.:

Susan McDermott

Senior Editor (Professional/Trade Division)

AFP Staff:

Jan Alfieri

Manager, New Product Development

Rhonda Starr

Vice President, Education and Training

This book is dedicated to the hundreds of
thousands of people who gave generously
of their time, money, and volunteer efforts
to help rebuild New Orleans following
Hurricane Katrina. All of us who
experienced the outpouring of support shown
by so many private groups and individuals
from around the globe remain forever grateful.

Contents

Contents

Contents

Contents

Acknowledgments

Thanks first to my clients, past and present, for all your wonderful ideas, advice, and support, including: The New Orleans Museum of Art, the Louisiana SPCA, Xavier University, the National World War II Museum, Neighborhood Housing Services, my favorite New Orleans charter schools, Newman School, and Metairie Park Country Day School, among others. I have learned more from all of you than I can ever give back. A special thanks to Jan Alfieri and her committee at AFP for keeping me on their author roster. I also owe a big debt of gratitude to my editors at John Wiley and Sons, Brandon Dust, Susan McDermott, and Lisa Vuoncino, for getting my manuscript in shape and keeping it on the right track.

This book is dedicated to my patient and loving family: to Cedric for doing all the computer back-ups, to Ben for creating my web site, and especially to Jacob, who carefully edited every chapter (no more semicolons, I promise!). I couldn't have done it without all of you.

About the Author

Julia Ingraham Walker holds a BA and an MA in English from Tulane University and an MBA from Rollins College in Florida. Her initial marketing expertise was gained during 10 years as a professional in college admissions, first at Tulane and then as Director of Admissions at Rollins. In 1985, she returned to New Orleans and began a career in fundraising that has spanned 25 years and numerous positions ranging from directing the annual fund to major gifts.

In 1990, Ms. Walker was appointed Vice President for Institutional Advancement at her alma mater, Tulane, where she served until 1998. In this position she supervised more than 100 employees in the advancement area and directed the university's $250 million capital campaign. Tulane's campaign raised over $75 million for the school's endowment and provided the resources for the construction or major renovation of eight campus buildings. In 1994, Ms. Walker was named Outstanding Fundraising Executive by her peers in the New Orleans chapter of AFP, the Association of Fundraising Professionals.

Ms. Walker has been active as an independent fundraising consultant since 1998 and has conducted and advised campaigns that total more than $700 million. Her clients include a wide range of nonprofits, from museums and schools to grassroots community organizations. She has helped to manage capital campaigns for clients in the fields of religion, health care, the arts, historic preservation, low-income housing, K-12 education, higher education, and research. Her areas of expertise include campaign feasibility studies, campaign planning and implementation, and nonprofit management, including management and training of nonprofit staff, volunteers, and boards.

Ms. Walker is a member of AFP and has participated in numerous national conferences and workshops on fundraising topics. She has published two prior fundraising books with John Wiley & Sons, *Nonprofit Essentials: The Capital Campaign*, and *Nonprofit Essentials: Major Gifts*. Post-Katrina, she returned home to New Orleans and has been assisting nonprofits in the region to reopen, recover, and rebuild.

Ms. Walker can be reached through her web site, www.walkercapital campaigns.com, and would welcome any comments or suggestions from readers of this book.

Introduction

What's money? A man is a success if he gets up in the morning and goes to bed at night and in between does what he wants to do.

Bob Dylan, singer and songwriter (1941–)

As I write this introduction, difficult economic times have fallen on all of us who work in the not-for-profit sector. Money is tight and donors are cautious. Endowments have lost value and fundraising goals are harder to reach. If your organization has already started a fundraising campaign, you may be finding that the going is tough. If you are planning a campaign, you may be worried about what to expect, and you would be right. These are times to move forward with caution, but standing still isn't a viable option for most of us.

This book is meant to provide a process for learning how to identify problems, regroup, initiate positive changes, and move ahead with your campaign in order to achieve success.

Almost all fundraising campaigns, even in the best of economic times, experience difficulties and slowdowns at various points along the way. The problems that trip up campaigns are often similar from one organization to another. Many of these issues are predictable and can be resolved with the assistance and advice of an experienced campaign consultant. My intent in writing this book is to share with you my own experiences, gleaned from dozens of campaigns, so that you can diagnose and treat your own campaign, rebuild momentum, and get your fundraising back on track.

Fundraising campaigns are among the most complex initiatives that any organization can undertake. A campaign requires substantial advance planning, brilliant research skills, an exciting reason to give, a split-second sense of timing, and superlative people skills. Those who lead campaigns must have courage, perseverance, excellent communication skills, and rely on a great sense of humor to live through it all. Add to that the need to perform in an unprecedented and difficult economic environment, and you can see that this is not a task for the faint of heart.

Why have a campaign at all? There is more to a fundraising campaign than just raising money (although the money is important). There is no other group activity in the nonprofit world that brings the whole organization together and moves it forward like a successful, well-run campaign. For creating excitement, building momentum, and making progress towards goals, the campaign is an unparalleled experience. A successful campaign brings together the organization's diverse constituents, focuses on an identified set of needs, and leaves the organization stronger and more resilient than it was before the campaign began.

How do you jump-start a stalled campaign? This book is full of strategies, tips, stories, and techniques to help you move your campaign out of the doldrums. I hope that you enjoy the ride, and please contact me if you have comments or suggestions about the advice in this book. I can be reached through my web site, www.walkercapitalcampaigns.com, and I look forward to hearing from you.

Real success is finding your lifework in the work that you love.

David McCullough, biographer and historian (1933–)

JUMP-STARTING THE STALLED FUNDRAISING CAMPAIGN

CHAPTER 1

Fundraising in a Challenging Economic Environment

 After reading this chapter, you will be able to:

- Understand the new environment for giving.
- Take immediate steps to shore up your fundraising programs.
- Identify the Top 10 campaign mistakes and how to avoid them.
- Create a more efficient advancement operation.

A New Environment for Philanthropy

Suddenly things have gotten a lot tougher in the fundraising business. What began as a credit crisis on Wall Street has become a full-fledged global recession. Investment scandals have rocked the foundation world. Nonprofits have begun searching for new ways to make budgets stretch further, to do more with less, and to maximize their return on investment.

Many organizations already in campaign mode are finding their momentum has slowed down, either because people are not giving at all or because donors who are still loyal are making smaller gifts. Some campaigns are slashing staff and budgets. Some organizations are pushing back campaign timetables to wait for better times. What can you do to strengthen your campaign and find the support your organization needs in tough times?

This book is a guide to help you develop a strategic approach to fundraising in a weak economy. In this chapter, you will find out how to tell if your campaign is in trouble, what short-term steps you can take to stem your losses, and how to avoid the Top 10 campaign mistakes. The final section of this chapter guides you on how to make the advancement operation more efficient, including some ideas for cutting costs.

The chapters that follow will help you take stock of the current environment for giving, take steps to help your fundraising programs over the long term, and retool your campaign with new strategies to take advantage of current economic and market realities.

Fundraising Angst

Historically, overall charitable giving has tended to weather the ups and downs of the stock market fairly well. In an article dated November 25, 2008, the *Wall Street Journal* notes: "In the past, charitable giving has tended to withstand economic turmoil."

The article then goes on to explain, however, why this downturn is different, explaining that foundations are seeing hard times: ". . . some foundations are cutting budgets by up to 20 percent or borrowing . . . to fulfill multiyear commitments," says Steven Gunderson, president and CEO of the Council on Foundations.

The news about corporate giving is not any better: "Many corporate funders are really going to be putting a freeze on any sort of new commitments and new initiatives," says Melissa Berman, president of Rockefeller Philanthropy Advisers.

All of this bad news is producing fundraising angst among charities and advancement professionals. Given the startling devaluation of assets in the markets over the past year, a loss of donors should hardly be a surprise. We can predict longer term issues, too: If a donor's asset levels drop, the donor's gift size will most likely drop.

To quote Maurice R. "Hank" Greenberg, the former chairman of AIG, whose Starr Foundation assets suffered a 50 percent decline, falling to $1.5 billion from about $3 billion over the past two years: "You can't give what you haven't got" ("Charitable Gifts from Corporations Fall Amid Slump," published in the *Wall Street Journal*, November 25, 2008).

IN THE REAL WORLD

"The Outlook is Grim"

The Chronicle of Philanthropy reported on December 15, 2008, that "the outlook is grim for many charities now entering the final weeks of the year when giving normally increases sharply. . . . In a *Chronicle* spot-check of donations to 35 charities, 28 organizations said that giving is flat or down this calendar year, and 10 are reporting declines of 10 percent or more."

The Wall Street Journal quoted a survey released by the Center on Philanthropy at Indiana University in an article dated December 22, 2008, ("After Madoff, Donors Grow Wary of Giving"): ". . . almost 94 percent of nonprofit professionals reported that the economy is having a 'negative' or 'very negative' effect on fundraising."

Most individuals give out of income (as opposed to giving out of assets) for annual gifts and small capital gifts, which might provide hope for giving in a time when investments have taken the brunt of the drop in market value. However, now it appears that smaller gifts made from income will be affected, too, as middle and lower income donors lose their jobs or find their income declining. For these donors, we will have to wait and see how the economic winds blow to determine whether they will still be making charitable gifts, even in small amounts.

There are a few optimists, including Robert F. Sharpe Jr., president of the Sharpe Group, a fundraising firm in Memphis. Quoted in the *New York Times*, Mr. Sharpe pointed to historical trends showing that philanthropy has remained strong in past recessions and even during the Great Depression. "Just about any way you look at it, the Depression was one of the best periods for charitable fundraising," Mr. Sharpe told the *Times* (November 11, 2008) in "Bracing for Lean Times Ahead." The *New York Times* article goes on to discuss the opinions of Patrick M. Rooney of the Center on Philanthropy at Indiana University, who also sounds fairly bullish on giving:

> The most reliable indicator of individual giving was Standard & Poor's 500 stock index, with a 100-point jump translating into an additional $1.5 billion of philanthropy from people who report donations on tax forms. "It works just the same way on the downside," Rooney said, predicting that individual giving will drop far less than the financial markets have fallen.

While we can hope for the best, unfortunately, the current economic woes have hit fundraisers with a double whammy. Key assets that might have shored up a donor's financial health in earlier recessions, such as real estate and investments, have declined precipitously. At the same time, current income and job stability have been affected negatively in industries across the world. We do not really know how donors will respond over the long term to the current economic environment, because this economic downturn is the first one that involves a global economy.

KEY CONCEPT

We are entering an unprecedented period of global economic recession when past giving patterns may not be predictive of future giving.

Some nonprofits also face formidable issues from financial threats that reach beyond fundraising. Many nonprofits receive a portion of their annual income from their endowments (funds where the principal has been invested and only a portion of the interest income is spent each year). Because investment values have fallen, institutional endowments are down, meaning that the income from endowments will also fall. Many of our organizations rely on endowment income to balance our budgets, and with this source of income down, cuts will have to be made in other areas.

IN THE REAL WORLD

Losses in Endowment Values

Many nonprofit institutions have suffered huge losses in their endowments. The *Wall Street Journal* reports:

> Donors may have reason to be concerned. Aside from the losses allegedly sustained by nonprofits in the Madoff mess, foundation endowments nationwide have lost 30 percent of their value, or about $200 billion, since the Dow Jones Industrial Average peaked in October 2007, according to the Council on Foundations, a trade group based in Alexandria, Virginia. Yale University, for example, recently estimated its endowment, which holds many illiquid assets such as real estate and private-equity investments, has fallen 25 percent since June 30. The school, higher education's second-richest, said its endowment now stands at about $17 billion, down from $22.9 billion on June 30.
>
> "After Madoff, Donors Grow Wary of Giving,"
> *Wall Street Journal*, December 22, 2008

Other sources of dependable income may also be affected as families absorb financial losses. Private school tuition may prove difficult for many families to afford. Patients who lose health care benefits may be unable to afford medical care, putting our health care institutions at a greater risk. Providing funding support for the arts and cultural sector may come to be viewed as a lower priority than supporting those sectors viewed as necessary, such as education, housing, crime prevention, and health services.

Meanwhile, the services that our nonprofits provide are being taxed with increased demand. Food banks and shelters are already experiencing longer lines and a growth in clientele. Universities are seeking to increase scholarship funds to meet increased student and family need. Government cuts in many programs have increased the demand for private support of services such as community health care, job training, and early childhood education.

The problems we face are real. This economic downturn is affecting our institutions differently than previous downturns. We are all facing serious threats to the financial stability of our nonprofit organizations and finding fewer places to turn to meet our needs. The purpose of this book is to give you some strategies for dealing with the downturn by repositioning your organization, creating plans to sustain giving, and focusing on new strategies for getting your campaign back on track.

Is Your Campaign in Trouble?

The purpose of this book is to help you and your organization weather the storm. To learn how your campaign stacks up, take the quiz in Exhibit 1.1. If yours is a troubled campaign, the ideas presented in this book should help you rebuild your fundraising efforts, restructure your campaign, and regain momentum. If you are considering launching a campaign, you can learn how to avoid the pitfalls described here.

EXHIBIT 1.1

Is Your Campaign in Trouble?

Answer the following questions with a yes or no response. Give one point for a ''yes'' answer and two points for a ''no'' answer. Add up your points and check the key on the following page to see where your campaign ranks.

1. Has your campaign raised less money in the past six months than in the six-month period preceding that?

2. Has the number of solicitation calls made each month declined over the past six months?

3. Are your volunteers beginning to delay making calls, fearing rejection?

4. Are your prospects telling you that they are giving to other needs that are more pressing than yours?

5. Have you given up on ever getting your top gift level met?

6. Have you begun to think about dropping the levels for donor recognition?

---

7. Are your campaign leaders burned out?

8. Is your case feeling stale when you make it to prospects?

9. Have you run out of new prospects?

10. Do you often feel like you want to look for a new job?

Key:

10 to 12 points: You might need a new job, but read this book first. Your campaign is in big trouble.

13 to 16 points: Your campaign might succeed if you change the way you are doing things. Hold that resume.

17 to 20 points: Maybe you should write a book. Your campaign is doing well and you can teach others how to hold up their end in fundraising.

If your campaign is in trouble, you are not alone, so do not take the problems personally. Even in good times, campaigns run into problems. Issues revolving around timing, donor recognition, and sight-raising plague most campaigns. The solutions to these problems can be applied to help your campaign move forward, even in a tough environment.

There are a number of ways that advancement professionals can influence the direction of their fundraising outcomes. It is important to realize that longer term strategies to fix a stalled campaign take time to identify, test, and implement. In this book, we present a strategic and long-term approach to retooling your campaign. There may be short-term steps to take first, however, before you begin addressing your campaign challenges.

Take Immediate Steps to Shore up Your Fundraising Programs

While you undertake the in-depth analysis that is required to rebuild your campaign (see Chapter 2), there are some immediate steps you can take to shore up your fundraising. Consider implementing some or all of these options right away:

1. ***Do not hit the panic button.*** We do not know how deep and how long this recession will be. Take a deep breath and make some plans to help your institution get through this period with the best possible outcomes.

2. ***Tighten up your case.*** Your donors need to know how important your programs and services are. Back up your case with new statistics and show how the current economic situation is affecting your programs as you meet increased needs.

3. ***Stretch out your timetable.*** If you are in a campaign, add another six months to a year to the timetable. Offer donors longer pledge periods if their jobs have been affected by the crisis. Reevaluate timing on big asks for the moment. Even wealthy donors feel poor when their assets drop by 30 percent or more.

4. ***Focus on the annual fund.*** Keep unrestricted funds for operations coming in so your institution's cash flow is healthy, and focus on keeping donors. Just getting all of last year's donors to give at the same level this year should be considered a victory.

5. ***Improve communications.*** Keep communications open inside and outside your institution. Inform donors about how the changes in the economy are affecting you and those you serve. Consider brief e-mail updates, web conferencing, or other crisis communication techniques.

6. ***Strengthen your planned giving program.*** Donors might not be able to give large gifts out of current assets, but bequests and trusts are options they can implement while hanging on to their assets for now.

7. ***Do not fire the advancement staff.*** This is the time when your organization needs loyal, hard-working people who will stay on top of the situation. Advancement professionals should keep their profile high to earn the trust of those around them. Make the advancement office part of the solution, not part of the problem.

8. ***Keep in touch with top level prospects and donors.*** It may be that some of your top prospects and donors are not able to make new gifts or even pay

on pledges, due to financial losses. Work with them individually, and do not forget that what goes around comes around. When the economy improves, donors will remember who stood by their side.

Employ Crisis Management Techniques

In many ways, navigating through the current fundraising situation is like working through a crisis. Your first steps must be to open communication channels, to keep staff focused on the work at hand, and to prevent panic by remaining calm and in control.

Keeping the organization together, or basic organizational survival, is the second step in crisis management. Organizational survival may call for taking some immediate tough measures. If you are involved in these decisions, take the lead by pushing for a quick summary analysis of the fiscal situation before any action is taken.

Your chief financial officer should help determine where your organization stands financially. If you are working in advancement, you can help by providing adjustments to projections for campaign revenue, annual fund receipts, and other ongoing giving programs. Perhaps in addition to a decline in fundraising, there are other departments that have had trouble meeting budgeted goals.

Find out how deep and how fast cuts have to be made just to keep your doors open. Then take stock, plan for some measures for survival, and communicate them across the board to all of your constituents. Measures for survival might include taking tough actions to staunch losses. Here are some ideas for immediate measures to take across the entire organization:

- Freeze open positions to help cut costs.
- Halt new construction and movement on new programs.
- Cut back or delete the annual raise pool.
- Fall back on cash reserves or other sources of income held in reserve.
- Move to increase earned income wherever possible.

The third phase of crisis management, after shoring up the survival of the organization, is to make new long-term plans for the organization. This may include small or large changes to the structure, staffing, and goals of the organization. The end result after this phase may be an organization that does not look exactly like what you started with.

Your job in advancement is to absorb these changes into your own department's outlook and to determine how they affect fundraising outreach, planning, and staffing. Then you must find ways to communicate the changes to your outside constituents, especially in your campaign. The campaign's needs, goals, and timetable may all change as the organization changes. The flexibility to think ahead and plan for new challenges is exactly the skill needed for fundraising professionals who want to succeed in this difficult environment.

Take a Hard Look at Your Campaign

After you have implemented some of the immediate fundraising recommendations discussed previously, take a hard look at your campaign. This may require taking a short campaign time-out. You will need time to analyze and review campaign results, assess changes in campaign structure and timing, and to identify and cultivate new prospects.

The first step in fixing a broken or stalled campaign is to learn what went wrong. The external environment is difficult, granted, but that only means that you cannot afford to make any errors. The current fundraising environment is not going to grant you any room for mistakes.

There are many mistakes common to campaigns all over the country that can delay or hurt your fundraising progress. We will take a brief look at the 10 most common of these in this section and offer some ideas on how to correct them (see Exhibit 1.2). Later chapters of this book will give you a more detailed outline for how to analyze your campaign, what to fix, and how to build on your strengths.

EXHIBIT 1.2

The Top 10 Campaign Mistakes

1. Not asking for a large enough leadership gift at the top of the gift table.

2. Not identifying and cultivating enough prospects to meet your needs.

3. Weak leadership from board and/or campaign leaders.

4. Asking too soon.

5. Not asking at all.

6. Not closing the solicitation once it has been made.

7. Taking donors for granted once a gift is closed.

8. Going back to the same old donors over and over.

9. Not energizing your constituents at all levels on your behalf.

10. Not developing a strong enough case to show why you need the money.

Let's review the issues raised in Exhibit 1.2 in more detail to understand them better:

1. *Lowering the leadership gift size.*

Many campaign planners now presume that top level gifts will be smaller than leadership gifts received by the organization in the past. Do not downsize your top gift expectations until they are tried and proven to be too high. With many prospects, we do not know yet which assets have been affected in what manner, so making assumptions could be a mistake. Use enhanced recognition options, gift matches and challenges, or planned giving tools to raise the level of your top gift. It is much easier to raise one large gift in this economy than many small ones! Do not be afraid of asking for more at the top.

2. *Identifying too few prospects.*

Yes, your campaign will need to identify new prospects. First, make sure that you are treating your current donors well (see mistake 7). Then invest in some prospect research techniques, including new ones like electronic prospect screening. Do not dismiss older, more personal methods of screening, like holding screening and rating sessions with supporters. Carry a prospect list with you to all meetings and ask donors to review it—you can never tell when someone close to you will have a connection to a distant prospect.

3. *Weak board or campaign leadership.*

Now is the time for board and campaign leaders to stand up and be counted. Your leaders need to take charge by addressing key financial issues, cutting back if necessary, and taking part in the reassessment of your campaign. This also means ensuring they give to their level of capability and continuing to ask them to open the door to others who can give. Make your board members part of the solution—inform them, involve them, and give them important tasks to do.

4. *Asking too soon.*

Some organizations have a short-term approach to cultivation and campaign giving. They roll through prospect lists like a steamroller, extracting the gifts that are easily available and balking at donors with more complex demands. Take time to cultivate. There is a better chance of getting a higher gift level if the prospect truly understands your needs. Do not rush large gifts. It may be more important to wait and get a big gift next year than to close a small one right now.

5. *Not asking at all.*

We have all seen campaigns that never get to the point. A prospect is cultivated, cultivated, and cultivated without an ask ever being made. This is not respectful to the needs of the organization, to the volunteers, or even to the donor. Decide when enough is enough, and cut to the chase. Making an ask can be tough, but spending all that time and money on a prospect with nothing to show for it is just not productive.

6. *Weak closing skills.*

Work with your volunteers, staff, and executive director/CEO on their skills, especially in asking for and closing a gift. Too many solicitors lose their focus during the last segment of a solicitation call and fail to get a gift closed. There are real techniques to learn here, so plan a workshop or do role playing to bring everyone up to speed. You have invested so much in getting a prospect to the point of an ask, do not let your staff or volunteers fail when it comes time to close the gift.

7. *Taking donors for granted.*

We have included a whole section on donor stewardship in this book (see Chapter 3). Treating current donors well means more than writing a thank-you letter. Keep your donors informed and involved, and they will keep giving back. It costs much less to return to a prior donor for a gift than it does to find, cultivate, and solicit a new prospect. Implement a strong stewardship program and it will pay you back many times over.

8. *Going back to the same old donors.*

See mistake 2 on page 11. If you are only soliciting prior donors, your organization will die on the vine. New constituents are the lifeblood of any organization. If you cannot figure out how to reach new groups, consider developing a partnership with another organization in your community that has the kind of audience you would like to reach. Offer to trade lists, to combine asks, or to develop programs together to cement your partnership. Be creative about outreach to younger donors; try social networking or viral campaigns to broaden your base.

9. *Not energizing constituents.*

If your campaign needs are truly urgent, your constituents at all levels need to share that sense of urgency. Create energy for your campaign by harnessing new electronic communication methods like interactive web sites and social networking, develop public events to showcase your services, and create a new PR plan to build support for your cause. Find ways to get people talking about your organization and create a buzz. Study the Obama campaign's strategy of building a broad, energized base of support through regular e-mail communication. Ask your supporters to do something to help your cause, such as watching a video, forwarding a message to friends, or making a small donation.

10. *Presenting a fuzzy case.*

It can be surprising how weak some campaigns are when it comes to making their case. "Because we need it," is not a case. "We are doing good work," is not a case. Make sure that your case answers questions like these: Why should I give? What are the needs I can give to? How urgent are these needs? What will happen if I do not give now? What impact will my gift have? Spend more time sharpening your case to stand out in the crowd and you will improve your fundraising results exponentially.

Each of these points represents key areas of campaign knowledge that will be developed further in the chapters that follow. You will learn specific techniques and tips, and see examples of how to counter problems like those identified above. Now it is time to plan a time-out so that you can get started on the analysis and planning effort that will help get your campaign back on track.

Take Time Out while You Plan

Putting things on hold in the middle of a campaign runs against basic fundraising instincts. Momentum is the heart of a strong campaign, and taking a decision to slow the momentum seems counterintuitive. Your gifts have probably slowed considerably already or your campaign would not be in a slump. There are good reasons for taking a short time-out from the campaign to get things in order.

The first step toward restarting the stalled campaign is to conduct or commission an in-depth analysis of funds raised to date (see Chapter 2 for specifics).

Movement forward from this point should be based on a set of strategies to be developed using the results of the campaign analysis. To keep pushing now, without the proper plan in place, will not help the outcome improve.

There are several reasons for calling a campaign time-out when fundraising results begin to slow down. It is very important when the going gets tough that advancement professionals work smarter, not harder. Pushing ahead against a brick wall will simply exhaust everyone and burn out staff and volunteers alike.

The campaign time-out can last any amount of time you need, from two months to two years. Three to six months is probably a good range to consider. Calling a campaign time-out offers the following benefits:

- Additional time to focus on campaign analysis.

- Additional time to develop new strategies.

- Time for longer term planning such as campus planning or facility planning to identify future needs.

- Time to allow donors to take stock of their finances.

- Time for prospects to reassess their giving strategies, especially foundations and corporations that have suffered significant losses in annual giving budgets.

- Time to work with your board and volunteers on new campaign strategies.

- Time to identify and cultivate new prospects.

- Time to reassess the advancement budget and staff and downsize if needed.

KEY CONCEPT

Taking a campaign time-out will allow you the time needed to identify and implement new strategies to put your campaign back on track.

Be sure to include your board and senior administration in your decision to take a campaign time-out. Board and campaign leaders may have mixed reactions to hitting the pause button. Some may feel that momentum will be lost or crucial dollars missed out on by not continuing aggressive action in the campaign.

The truth is that if your campaign is lagging, it has already lost its momentum. If dollars are not coming in at the desired level to meet your stated needs, you already have a stalled campaign. Pretending it is not so will not help the situation. The best response is to stop, identify the issues, determine how to address them, and then develop a plan to reinvigorate the campaign.

TIPS AND TECHNIQUES

How to Talk to Your Board about a Campaign Time-Out

- Line up your arguments ahead of time. Do not make them up as you go.
- Use facts, such as decreased participation levels or decreased gift sizes, to shore up your argument.
- Ask board members to talk about their experiences with other campaigns across your community. Yours is hardly the only organization affected by sluggish results.
- Explain how you will use the time-out: to analyze your results to date, to identify strengths and weaknesses in your campaign, and to come back with new strategies for this environment.
- Set a specific time frame, such as eight weeks, for the time-out period.
- Involve your campaign leaders in the answer: Suggest that the board and campaign leadership hold a retreat after the campaign analysis has been concluded. Present them with a summary of the analysis and ask them to help you formulate strategies to turn around the campaign.
- Share information fully, even bad information. Your board and administrative management will trust you if they always hear the whole truth from you. Do not hide bad results—use them as a reason to stop, analyze, and strategize.

Improving Advancement Efficiency: Campaign Staffing and Budgets

Advancing in the Face of Downsizing

It is not always a good strategic move to make cuts to the advancement team. In the long run, cutting the advancement operation will hurt the entire organization if fewer resources are raised for all as a result. As all experienced development people know: *It takes money to raise money.*

How can you make the case for spending on advancement? Try to mount a good rationale for keeping (or even increasing) advancement resources by taking the lead in conversations about the economy, sharing knowledge about the funding community, and providing a plan for how to move forward. Create a table that shows the historic relationship between dollars spent on advancement and dollars raised over the past 5 to 10 years. Keep visible with senior level managers and board members. Make them look to you for answers. Become indispensable as the interpreter of what is happening externally to those who are struggling internally.

Know and defend your cost per dollar raised. In many campaigns, the cost per dollar raised is surprisingly low; many independent schools, community nonprofits, and museums spend from 3 cents to 10 cents per dollar on their campaign activities. At universities, which often have larger and more sophisticated fundraising teams, the average cost runs between 10 cents and 20 cents for every dollar raised. Use good data from your own organization to help make a strong case that investment now will pay off for the organization later.

Review Advancement Staff and Budget

There is no question that the challenges of the current economic environment will pressure nonprofits to cut overhead. In the long run, this is not always a bad thing. Staff members get added, programs become more complex, and goals are set higher in good times. It is only natural to expect that the pendulum will swing back. But how can you still run your campaign with less staff and/or a smaller budget?

There are many ways to keep a campaign going on limited resources. Some of these ideas may even strengthen your campaign. Let us review some methods for saving money that can be effective in any campaign right away.

Methods for Cutting Campaign Costs:

1. *Stop printing campaign brochures.* Buy pocket folders, attach your logo to the front as a sticker, and fill it with materials created in-house and copies of local PR articles describing your organization. Donors will be thrilled to see that their gifts are not being spent on fancy printed materials.

2. *Develop a PowerPoint presentation that can be used in solicitations.* Make one great presentation and add video and music to help tell your story. Then personalize the presentation for each major campaign ask. Burn it onto a CD and leave it behind after a call, so the prospect can show it to his family or to his trustees.

3. *Move more campaign information to your web site.* Create a campaign page, or a whole new campaign web site with a link to your home page. Add a video showing the most recent campaign event. Put up blueprints, stories about gifts made, and profiles of the users of your services. Then start directing traffic to the web site by referring to it in all of your materials.

4. *Bring down the cost of campaign events.* Think smaller, as in intimate cultivation events for four or five couples hosted by volunteers at their homes. Ask the hosts to help out by paying for the expenses. Tap corporate volunteers for the use of their boardrooms for local campaign events. Ask volunteers to pay for their own travel to out of town events.

5. *Cut back on travel.* Many out of town donors will respond to e-mail, phone calls, and even the rare personal letter. Think about ways to hold down the cost for events out of town, like using a donor's club instead of a restaurant for a gathering. Do not stay in expensive hotels; instead, look up an old friend or even a donor you like and ask to use their guest bedroom.

6. *Ask volunteers to do more.* Volunteers can be difficult to manage, but those who care about your organization's success are worth their weight in gold. Teach them new skills, bring them into your planning meetings, and keep them active on your side. You will need them.

KEY CONCEPT

Try outsourcing selected campaign functions to lower the overhead and cut back on the number of full-time staff.

Outsourcing works well for industry because it saves on benefits, keeps the business from paying its staff through downturns, and provides expertise only when it is needed. Consider doing the same thing with some of your campaign staffing functions. These are areas that can be outsourced while still preserving quality and functionality:

- *Prospect research:* Researchers are most valuable at the beginning of the campaign and when retooling in the middle. Keeping a full-time research office open through the ups and downs of the entire campaign timeline may not be necessary. Research skills can be bought by the hour from consultants or from moonlighting specialists working for another nonprofit.

- *Direct mail:* Direct mail has become so specialized that hiring a consultant who does this work full-time will usually produce better results than bringing it in-house. Find an experienced firm or ask your peers who they use.

- *Proposal writing:* Many advancement pros prize their proposal writing skills, but this is one area where a skilled outsider can deliver high quality work efficiently. Either a consultant or a part-timer can fill this need while you go see prospects. And you only need to pay them when you need a proposal.

- *Volunteer training and management:* Volunteers become more useful as budgets tighten, but they often need training and oversight. Use your campaign consultant to do this task, or better yet, find an experienced volunteer and pay her part-time to work with her peers.

- *Planned giving:* Try working with one of the large national planned giving consulting groups. They supply everything from printed newsletters to web site links that feature interactive giving planners. And you do not have to worry that they might not know the law—these people are the experts.

- *Event planning:* Campaign events can be a huge time suck, and they often distract from important cultivation and solicitation activities. Consider hiring an event planner or ask an experienced volunteer to manage events for you.

Work Smarter, Not Harder

The addition of outside experts allows you to focus on what you and your staff do best, which should be representing your organization in the best possible way to prospects and donors. Personal time spent with prospects is even more important now that you need every supporter on board. Use your time wisely by developing strategies, building relationships, and keeping major donors in the fold, rather than spending days in the office doing research or writing. Identify the major functions that can be moved away from full-time staff and focus on making the best use of the staff you have.

Summary

We do not know for how long the economy will remain in a recession, but certainly it provides challenges for the immediate future. You will want to refocus your campaign by developing new strategies to help your organization move forward in the face of a difficult environment. Employ some of the short-term techniques presented here for dealing with the crisis, and then take a time-out to plan for an overall strategic approach.

You can help your institution weather the storm by becoming familiar with the Top 10 campaign mistakes and learning how to avoid them. Plan with your board and staff members to take a campaign time-out while you correct mistakes and develop strategies to improve your fundraising results.

Learn how to make a strong case for spending on the advancement enterprise. While it still takes money to raise money, you can make your advancement operation more efficient by cutting costs and outsourcing selected staff functions.

Tough times call for more flexibility in your approach to problem-solving. Think creatively, draw on the creative energy of your staff, and use this as a period to try out new ideas. Embrace change, and both your attitude and your ability to work with those around you will improve.

CHAPTER 2

Looking Beneath the Surface: Analyze Campaign Results

After reading this chapter, you will be able to:

- Understand the fundraising patterns within your campaign.
- Evaluate your campaign's strengths and weaknesses.
- Adjust the campaign gift table to match new giving realities.

Analyze Fundraising Patterns

With all the focus on the difficulties of raising money during a period of economic distress, it can be difficult to get any perspective on your own campaign. Understanding the environment is only half the battle. Now you must look inside and understand your own campaign. In order to respond strategically to the challenges you face, you must first delve into what is working and what is not working with your fundraising efforts.

Learning what works requires a head-to-toe analysis of your gifts, solicitations, and strategies, starting from the beginning of the campaign. This analysis requires tapping into your institutional records for tracking and reporting on activities that have already taken place. The better your data has been kept, and the better your access to reports on that data, the easier it will be for you to perform the necessary analysis. If you must go back and recreate information with your staff, consider holding a retreat or planning day to do so. It may be helpful to engage the entire fundraising staff in the process.

For most advancement operations, all of the analytic work suggested here can be done in-house by internal staff. It may be preferable to identify one person to lead the process who can provide a fresh perspective on the campaign reports and results. If you feel that either the skills or the perspective are missing within your staff, consider hiring a consultant, borrowing a staff member from your finance office, or utilizing a volunteer with the appropriate skills.

 TIPS AND TECHNIQUES

Who Should Lead the Analysis of Your Campaign Results?

Select the best person available with the right skills:

- A senior advancement team member with systems skills.
- The chief advancement officer.
- A member of the accounting or finance staff.
- A trusted volunteer or board member.
- A consultant versed in campaigns.
- An experienced peer.

Analyze Giving Patterns

Campaign giving can be broken down into many different segments. You will want to look at all the different ways to break out and study the total giving your campaign has attracted to date.

KEY CONCEPT

The goal of analyzing the record of your campaign to date is to discover patterns that will help to identify the strengths and weaknesses of your fundraising activities.

It is important to keep the data as simple and clean as possible. While running multiple computer reports will be necessary, accuracy and clarity are the paramount virtues in this type of work. Whoever is chosen to lead the analysis should work personally with the staff members who run the data. It is all too easy to ask for one set of data and actually receive something else. Making the requests clear and succinct will result in better data. Avoid the GIGO effect: garbage in, garbage out.

These are the reports needed to analyze progress to date:

- All campaign donors by giving level.

- All campaign donors by geographic area.

- All campaign donors by giving purpose.

- All campaign donors by constituency, for instance, class year, parent, patient, and so forth.

- All campaign donors by source of funds: foundation, corporation, individual.

Sort the information requested by both the number of donors and the amount of dollars raised. When the reports arrive, take some time to study them in order to identify patterns of fundraising results. The more familiar the lead analyst becomes with the data, the more accurate the results will be.

The goal of analyzing the campaign data is to look for patterns that can help identify strengths and weaknesses resulting from campaign activity. The analyst wants to identify campaign activities that worked and those that did not work. The lead analyst should review the data with this goal in mind. As each report is reviewed, the analyst should jot down trends or patterns observed. Also note questions that arise as the results unfold. Sometimes questions raised can be useful in teasing out trends that are not obvious to the eye.

The analyst should note all observed patterns and conclusions, even if they are only preliminary. If conclusions are premature, they can be tested against further data points later in the process. A good analyst can instinctively tease out and identify trends that will determine which strategies worked best. Good analytical skills are part art and part science.

These are the five basic questions that the analyst should try to answer, and you might want to develop your own set of questions to add:

1. *How many gifts and how many dollars have been raised at each level?*

Giving levels may have already been defined in the campaign planning process with a preliminary gift table. If this was not done, then define gift ranges that are appropriate to your campaign, such as $10,000 to $24,999; $25,000 to $99,999; $100,000 to $249,999, and so on, up to the highest gift level achieved to date. Make a chart of the number of gifts at each level and the total dollars raised at each level, including the percentage of the total reached by gift level.

The end result will look just like a campaign gift table, but instead of illustrating the gifts that are sought after, it illustrates the gifts that have been raised. (See Exhibit 2.1 for a sample table of gifts received.)

2. *How many gifts and how many dollars have been raised from each geographic region?*

Define appropriate geographic regions for your organization if you have not already done so. Sort your giving in ways that makes sense for your campaign: by city, by zip code ranges, by region, or by state.

Preliminary analysis from a geographic perspective should answer these questions:

- Which geographic areas are strongest in terms of total giving (dollars)?
- Which geographic areas are strongest in terms of total giving (number of gifts)?

EXHIBIT 2.1

Table of Gifts Received for a $2 Million Campaign that Has Raised $1.3 Million

Gift Level	# of Gifts	Dollars	% of Total Raised
$500,000	1	$ 500,000	39%
$250,000	0	$ 0	0%
$100,000	2	$ 200,000	15%
$ 50,000	5	$ 250,000	19%
$ 25,000	6	$ 150,000	12%
$ 10,000	20	$ 200,000	15%
Total Raised		**$1,300,000**	**100%**

- Which geographic areas are weakest (in dollars and in gifts)?

- Which areas have produced the largest single gifts?

- Are there other observable patterns, for instance, more foundation gifts from one area, or more gifts for a specific purpose from one area?

The conclusions reached from a geographic analysis of gifts will help to define which areas to put the greatest amount of effort into going forward. The geographic reports might need to be requested based on the size of gift, purpose of the gift, and source of the gift, depending on the complexity of your information system and the types of data entered. This is where all those data entry hours pay off. Make sure the lead analyst uses the development information system to the fullest extent possible to discern information that might be useful.

3. *How many gifts and how many dollars have been raised for each giving purpose?*

In campaigns where there are multiple needs or divisions represented, it is important to understand which needs are attracting the most gifts and/or the largest gifts. This analysis will help to determine which purposes are most attractive to donors and which needs are not being met.

This analysis requires a sequence of reports that show:

- Giving to each school or division represented in the campaign.

- Giving to each program area in the campaign.

- In a comprehensive campaign, break out giving by endowment, program, operations, and capital needs.

Looking at the results to date, the campaign analyst might find, for instance, that the endowment portion of the campaign has fallen behind other areas in attracting the number of gifts needed. In order to correct this weakness, campaign leaders must first understand that endowment is the area that requires additional focus.

4. *How do gifts and dollars raised to date reflect the support of different campaign constituencies?*

Many nonprofit institutions have important constituent groups whose giving can be tracked and sorted for analysis. Universities and schools, for instance, usually track gifts from constituencies such as current parents, past parents, alumni (by class or decade), and current students. Hospitals look at former patients; museums track membership giving.

If you have not already done so, use this exercise to identify the major groups that have given to your campaign. Then look at giving patterns within each group. Compare historical data for giving from the period just before the campaign if it is available by group to discern trends over time.

What should you look for? Be on the alert to identify the following patterns:

- Classes or groups where the percentage of giving is especially high or low.

- Classes or groups where the total dollars given is especially high or low.

- Constituent groups that are growing stronger as the campaign progresses.

- Constituent groups that are getting weaker as the campaign progresses.

This analysis of giving by constituent groups will help lead the campaign leadership to conclude which groups need more attention and which groups might need a change in approach. For instance, if you discover that parents of current students are a giving constituency that is declining in participation as the campaign progresses, then you will want to develop special strategies to focus on improving the results from that group.

5. *What percentage of dollars raised has come from foundations, corporations, and individuals?*

All gifts come from an identifiable source of funds. The type of source—foundation, corporation, or individual—should be tracked in your campaign reports. If it has not been a part of your record keeping, go back and sort gifts by source from the beginning of the campaign, and begin to keep records on gift source.

In order to identify your campaign's best sources of funds moving forward, you must have a clear picture of where funds have come from in the past. For instance, if the campaign to date has raised only 20 percent of its funds from foundations, with 70 percent from individuals and 10 percent from corporate support, you might reach a preliminary conclusion that foundation and corporate fundraising could use a boost. Further review of prospects and giving patterns might prove or disprove this theory, but the first key step to strategizing future activities is to understand the patterns already developed.

Beware of the confusion between individuals, family foundations, and national foundations in identifying gift sources. Differentiate individuals who give through family foundations from individuals who give from income or assets, because their giving patterns will be entirely different from each other.

It is also useful to differentiate between local family foundations and large national foundations. (National foundations are giving entities that have professional boards and program advisors, such as the Ford Foundation, the Carnegie Corporation of New York, and the Andrew W. Mellon Foundation.) The distinction between local family foundations and large national foundations is useful because the process for decision making differs between local and national foundations.

Analyze Cultivation and Solicitation Patterns

After completing the reports that contain the data on donors and dollars, the lead analyst should review all available data on cultivation and solicitation activities since the beginning of the campaign. Again, the goal is to discern patterns of activity that brought in gifts vs. patterns of activity that were less successful.

The relative success or failure of campaign activities, such as cultivation steps and solicitation calls, are important to analyze because they represent areas over which you can exert some control. The purpose of cultivation steps is to bring the prospect closer to your organization. Cultivation steps should ultimately result in a gift. If a gift has not been asked for, or has not been closed, after a significant amount of cultivation activity, then you must make changes in either your campaign solicitation teams or in the timing of solicitation calls.

Using Moves Management to Track
Campaign Activity

Analysis of cultivation and solicitation activity requires installation of a prospect tracking program. Most development information systems now available contain packages for prospect tracking. This system of individually tracking all "moves" made on each prospect is referred to in advancement circles as "moves management." Ideally, each move—identified as a meaningful contact with the prospect—should be tracked and recorded in the system. Examples of prospect moves include such activities as attending events, having the prospect make visits to your site, making a personal cultivation call on the prospect, and making a solicitation call.

The reports based on prospect moves will allow your analyst to track which cultivation efforts lead to the most gifts. You will also find it useful to measure how much time it takes to move the average prospect from initial contact to closing the gift.

These are questions that might help to assess cultivation efforts:

- How many cultivation steps does it take to close the average gift?

- Is there a cultivation continuum (a series of meaningful contacts) that resulted in the most gifts?

- What is the average time it takes to move a prospect through cultivation and solicitation steps to the closing of the gift?

- Are there a large number of prospects who have been cultivated but who have not been asked for a gift?

- What percentage of prospects who were solicited actually made a gift?

The ability to tie cultivation patterns to solicitation patterns and the resulting outcomes in gifts closed is the activity at the core of the analytic exercise. Try to identify which solicitors (or teams of solicitors) have done the best job closing gifts. Measure the timing between the solicitation meeting and the closing of the gift. Be on the lookout for campaigns that cultivate, cultivate, and cultivate, but never ask; this is a common weakness of many campaigns. This pattern can be discerned by seeing a campaign with a large number of prospects who are linked to a large number of cultivation steps, but with few solicitations taking place. Most donors do not make a gift until they are asked.

 KEY CONCEPT

Tracking cultivation and solicitation moves with prospects will help you discover if asks are being made in a timely manner. Most donors do not make a gift until they are asked.

The reverse pattern is sometimes apparent: Campaigns can rush prospects to the ask without enough cultivation time. This pattern can be seen in records that show quick cultivation followed by a number of asks, but the majority of gifts closed will be smaller than expected.

Here are some questions to review about solicitation patterns:

- Which solicitor, or team of solicitors, has the best record in asking and closing gifts?

- Are there any indications that gifts are routinely coming in well below the ask level?

- Are there patterns of cultivation, solicitation, and gifts that differ between new donors and repeat donors?

It can be helpful to track cultivation and solicitation activity by whether the prospect has given to your institution before or is a new donor. New donors usually take longer to make gifts than repeat donors, because the new donors are still learning about your needs. Therefore more cultivation steps are required for first-time donors. New donors might also tend to give less, on average, with their first gift than repeat donors give.

Some development information systems can track entries for a prospect's rating, ask amount, and actual gift amount. Each prospect is thus linked to several dollar amounts: an initial estimate of capability (rating); the expected gift amount; the ask amount; and the actual gift amount. The use of all of these numbers helps to gauge how successful a solicitor has been in closing the highest possible gift.

Campaigns where the gifts that come in are always significantly lower than the ask levels, for example, may need to reassess their prospects' readiness for solicitation. They may be asking for the gift too soon in the process. It is also possible that some solicitors do a better job than others in keeping to the original ask amounts. Some solicitors leave the ask amount open, or lower the amount during the solicitation meeting due to various pressures. These are all patterns that are helpful to discern as you develop new strategies to fix your campaign.

Review Annual Fund Results

If you have not done so already, set up a weekly review with your institution's annual fund director. Have that individual break out the number of donors who are giving who are repeat donors, Lybunts (last year but not this year), Sybunts (some year but not this year), or new donors. Also look at whether the gift size has decreased from the level given by the same donor last year. This analysis of annual fund gifts will give you some sense of how donors are responding to solicitations from your organization even before campaign activity is added in.

How should you apply information gleaned from the annual fund program to your campaign? For example, let us say you learn that your organization has kept most of its annual fund donors from last year, but on the average those donors are giving less. You now know that loyal donors will give something, but the amount will probably be less. This fact can help you adjust campaign asks. Plan to go back to previous major donors for a campaign gift, but consider asking for less than the prior gift level.

Beyond the Advancement Office:
Measure Donor Engagement

Most donors do not interact solely with the advancement office in a nonprofit. Many prospects and donors make site visits, volunteer, read printed materials, peruse the web site, attend nondevelopment functions, talk to those whom the organization serves, and otherwise develop a relationship across the organization. All of these contacts affect prospects' perceptions of the organization's needs and ultimately influence their decision to give.

Most donors give because they are personally connected to or moved by the work of the organizations they give to. Engagement in the work of the nonprofit is traditionally a valuable way to cultivate prospects. You will want to determine whether personal engagement in the work of your organization is more or less important with your prospects. In order to do this, you must develop the ability to track volunteer work done by prospects within your organization.

To track contacts with prospects and donors beyond the advancement office, you will need to work with your colleagues across departmental lines to obtain the relevant information. First, find out if all the different ways in which a prospect might interact with your organization—especially through volunteer activity—are being tracked. If not, you might want to meet with volunteer program coordinators and develop such a tracking system. Your goal is to confirm the extent of involvement that your prospects and donors have with the organization across all programs.

These are the questions to answer relative to engagement with the organization:

- Does significant engagement with the organization result in more gifts?
- What level of activity between the donor and the nonprofit results in the most gifts (or the largest gifts)?
- Are there certain kinds of engagement activities that are more productive in producing donors?
- Can you enhance the engagement of prospects with the organization in order to produce more gifts?
- Are there methods of engagement that could be created for those who live far away and cannot engage with the work of the organization on a personal basis?

As you seek information from your colleagues, explain that you are reviewing all facets of interaction between prospective donors and the organization, from communication to volunteer activity. You may be surprised to learn that your donors have a much broader set of interactions with the organization than you thought previously.

Assessing the quality, depth and interest area of donors' relationships with the institution could provide important clues in your attempt to find patterns that lead to giving. This analysis can be a valuable key to help you learn how much, and how deeply, your prospects need to be involved in the work of your institution in order to participate generously as donors.

Evaluating Strengths and Weaknesses in Your Campaign

Successful campaign leaders learn what works and what does not work to turn prospects into donors for their institutions. This is why campaign data analysis is so important; you must first understand your successes and failures in order to implement change that works.

Once the analyst has completed a preliminary round of data review, and some of the basic patterns and trends of the campaign have been identified, it is time to make some decisions about what to fix and how to fix it. It is important to differentiate between strengths and weaknesses in the analysis of campaign results, because your goal now is to build on strengths.

Strategize Beyond Departmental Boundaries

There are a number of ways to interpret and act on the data that has been brought to light through the process you have just completed. Some advancement CEOs close the door, take out a pencil or a laptop, and make their own assessment about what should be done. Others turn the information developed over to a consultant and ask for help.

It can be a good idea to bring a fresh perspective to the problems of a stalled campaign, as long as the information gleaned is factored through a mind-set of what is possible to fix, along with an understanding of what went wrong. In order to best interpret the data and determine next steps, we recommend creating a working campaign group composed of experienced staff members and one or two new experts who can strategize together.

Now is not the time to burrow into the corner of the advancement office. In order to move forward effectively in a challenging environment, nonprofit leaders must harness all of their creative resources, along with available staff and budgets, to pull in the same direction. A time of scarce resources and shrinking donor pools is not the time for a silo mentality. It takes strong leadership to make management and staff members pull in the same direction, but this is a time when leadership can truly make a difference.

KEY CONCEPT

In times of economic distress, when tough choices have to be made, the best strategy is to put the greatest resources where the greatest returns are available.

We recommend instituting a midterm campaign planning group—let us call them the Campaign Fixers—that cuts across the substantial departmental barriers found at most organizations. Include the advancement CEO, the analyst who worked on the data, and the campaign director. Add a member of the staff who is familiar with prospects, such as a major gifts officer or a prospect researcher. Then draw from the best and most flexible minds available across the institution. This could include the finance VP, program directors, or the human resource director. You know who they are in your institution! Include at least one board member or campaign committee volunteer in your planning group, and make sure to add the communications or PR director to help with issues related to messaging and materials.

What is the goal of the Campaign Fixers? This group will become the strategists, the ones who will help move from data analysis to the creation of an action plan that can be implemented to achieve campaign success. The group can meet once, twice, or once a week until the planning effort is completed. It can meet in a retreat format or for lunch every day. Whatever structure you impose on your group, make sure that one member is assigned to write everything down. You may find yourself looking back for ideas that were generated in the earliest stages of the meeting after later concepts have been discarded.

IN THE REAL WORLD

Here is an example of a campaign building on strengths.

An art museum has a strong local donor base in the Midwestern city where it is located, but it also receives a few large contributions from New York City, where there exists an array of philanthropic organizations associated with the arts and cultural interests. The museum is in the quiet phase of a $50 million expansion campaign, but the campaign has slowed down significantly as the economy has weakened. Conducting a geographic analysis of giving showed that 80 percent of the campaign gifts to date came from the museum's home base, which we will call its primary market. Another 12 percent of the gifts came from New York City, which we would consider a secondary market for the museum.

Strategic question: Should the museum focus its campaign efforts where it has been most successful (closer to home, in its primary market) or increase its efforts in New York, its secondary market?

The decision facing the museum's campaign staff was whether the proper strategy was to build on their strong suit (local support), improve on their weaker flank (in New York), or try to do both. They based their strategy decision on the potential in their prospect pool. Because there continues to be substantial money available for the arts in New York, cutting back on all efforts there did not seem to be the best strategy for the long term. However, they agreed that their yield from New York efforts would not be realized in the short term. They also utilized relevant information—in this case, the financial meltdown among New York banks and investment houses—to delay the timing of their New York efforts.

The museum decided to focus on local donors over the next year but to continue cultivation of its New York prospects and to reassess their potential in New York in the following year. This gave their campaign a short-term focus on results without losing the long-term potential for new gifts from larger prospects down the line in New York. With this dual strategy, the team regained its momentum and kept the campaign moving toward success.

Build on Strengths

How do we identify our strengths? Strengths can be deduced from campaign results that show positive trends or patterns. Weaknesses are either the inverse, that is negative trends, or patterns that show poor results. A strength can also be defined as the mirror image of a weakness.

KEY CONCEPT

The most important advice for the Campaign Fixers is to build on identified strengths and minimize weaknesses.

The trick to turning around a failing campaign is to build on strengths, turn weaknesses into strengths, and create strategies that take advantage of things that are already working well. But be careful, because creating a strategy that works might not always be your first instinctive response to each problem identified!

In Exhibit 2.2, Example 1, for instance, we see a campaign that has one (and only one) highly successful solicitation team. An initial reaction might be to just pile more solicitations on the team that is getting good results. This would probably result in team burnout. Breaking the team up and pairing its members with others—the recommendation we are making here—has the advantage of reaching more prospects as well as training more volunteers to become stronger, experienced solicitors.

Sometimes the best strategy requires experimenting with the basic structure of gifts (Exhibit 2.2, Example 2). For this campaign, which is having an easier time raising capital gifts than gifts for endowment, we recommend including some portion of endowment as a part of each solicitation going forward. This organization could also consider going back to prior donors and asking each one to designate a portion of their capital gift to endowment. Note that turning this campaign around requires a complete restructuring of the solicitation technique, marking a serious strategic change to the campaign as a whole.

Referring again to Exhibit 2.2, Example 2, remember that only the donor can restrict a gift to endowment. Therefore, it is necessary to consult with each donor to gain permission to change the use of their gift (or a portion of their gift) in order to move it to endowment. Be sure to record the new gift designation in writing to avoid any misunderstandings.

Most organizations need to move beyond their core group of past donors when mounting a campaign. In Exhibit 2.2, Example 3, we see a campaign that is having trouble moving beyond this core group. The strategy we are recommending as a solution is to explore ways to ask the core group of committed donors to share their enthusiasm with new prospects. The additional strategy of asking for an extra year on pledges is a powerful way to reach higher goals by leveraging gifts already made to the campaign. In this case, we have taken a strength—the existence of a core group of loyal donors—and leveraged that strength to improve both outreach to new audiences and fundraising results.

Exhibit 2.2, Example 4 illustrates a problem common to many campaigns: how to reach a new and younger population regarding your cause? Communication techniques have changed substantially for younger people and traditional methods of reaching them, such as mailing them printed brochures, do not resonate with this group.

Save some money on printing and mount a viral campaign over the Internet to reach these prospects. (See Chapter 8 for an example of how a viral campaign is conducted in the real world.) Note that in the recommendation in Example 4, we took a campaign's weakness—motivating younger prospects—and turned it around into a strength by focusing on a new strategy to reach the targeted group.

With Exhibit 2.2, Example 5, we also attempt to turn an observed weakness into a strength. Campaign leaders should learn how to tap foundation and

---

EXHIBIT 2.2

Examples of Campaign Strengths and Weaknesses and Recommended Strategies Built in Response to Them

1. **Strength:** One team of solicitors outshines all the rest in terms of closing gifts.

   Weakness: There aren't enough good solicitors to cover the prospect pool.

   Strategy: Break up the A-team and couple each of the strong solicitors with a weaker solicitor to improve results overall and build more experienced teams.

   (Continued)

2. **Strength:** Most of the gifts that have come in have been given to capital needs.

   Weakness: Half of the campaign goal is to build endowment, and these gifts are lagging.

   Strategy: Consider asking all capital donors to designate a portion—as much as 20 percent—of their gifts to endowment. Develop a strong case for why endowment is necessary. Ask Board and Campaign Committee members to take this stance with their own gifts.

3. **Strength:** Most donors to the campaign are loyal, long-term donors to the organization.

   Weakness: This loyal cadre is small and has already committed their campaign gifts.

   Strategy: Take some of these loyalists on calls to visit new prospects who are less attuned to the organization. Take advantage of the loyalty by asking current donors to extend their gifts by one year; for example, on a five-year pledge add a sixth year, thus increasing their gift amounts by 20 percent.

4. **Strength:** Baby boomer donors (above age 50) have given the great majority of gifts.

   Weakness: Young constituents don't seem very involved, and most don't give.

   Strategy: Take a leaf from Barack Obama's campaign playbook. Create an exciting Internet-based campaign to communicate with younger people. Use e-mail to ask them to take small but meaningful steps toward involvement, such as forwarding a message to their peers, making a gift of $10, or watching a video.

5. **Strength:** The campaign has had great success with individual prospects.

   Weakness: Foundations and corporations have been relatively ignored.

   Strategy: This is one example where the weakness should be tackled head-on, since foundations and corporations represent potentially large sources of funding. Approach the issue strategically by working first on a strategy for foundations. Consider hiring a staff member or consultant well versed in this field, because it can take years to get up to speed on foundation giving. Find a good, experienced proposal writer. Be aware that foundations do not necessarily respond to campaign goals and activity, but will be more interested in the organization's mission, programs, achievements, and needs.

corporate prospects for their needs, even if they have been more successful with individual giving. While they have their own struggles in a weak economy, gifts from corporations and foundations can help to cushion ongoing weakness in the individual giving sector. A strong campaign should develop giving strategies for all three sectors—corporate, foundation, and individual giving—to provide a balance of risks and returns.

We will now look at difficulties that may arise with the original gift table as the campaign begins to slow down and how to make appropriate adjustments to meet the realities of gifts that are available.

Adjusting the Campaign Gift Table

Is your campaign missing leadership gifts at the top levels of your gift table? Patience is required with high level prospects as they adjust to the new economic realities. Wealthy prospects who have just lost 40 percent of the value of their stock portfolio are going to feel poor, even if they have millions left to give.

KEY CONCEPT

Do not give up on top level gifts in a weak economy. Step up ongoing cultivation to keep wealthy prospects aware of your needs.

If your campaign is missing prospects at the high end of the gift table, it is time to take a good look at strategies for prospects throughout the entire prospect pool. In times of economic weakness, your campaign may have to allow more time for high-end donors to be identified and cultivated or make do with more gifts at lower levels to reach its goals. Let us look at an example to see how complex this problem can be.

Look at the example of the campaign illustrated in Exhibit 2.3, where we have added additional columns to the table of gifts received that allow us to compare actual results to desired results.

EXHIBIT 2.3

Table of Gifts Received Compared with Gifts Needed

This table represents a $2M campaign that has raised $1.3M to date.

Gift Level	# Of Gifts In	# Additional Gifts Needed	$ Raised	$ Needed	% ($ Needed over $700,000)
$500,000	1	0	$ 500,000	$ 0	
$250,000	0	1	$ 0	$250,000	36%
$100,000	2	2	$ 200,000	$200,000	29%
$ 50,000	5	3	$ 250,000	$150,000	21%
$ 25,000	6	4	$ 150,000	$100,000	14%
$ 10,000	20	0	$ 200,000	$ 0	
Totals	**34**	**10**	**$1,300,000**	**$700,000**	**100%**

There is a real weakness in the top level gifts for this campaign. Based on this table of gifts received, the campaign in Exhibit 2.3 needs to raise one new gift at the $250,000 level and two gifts at the $100,000 level. These two gift levels together comprise over 60 percent of the funds that are missing. This campaign needs $700,000 more in gifts to reach its goal. How can these additional gifts be realized?

First, let us break down the results and reach some preliminary conclusions about strengths and weaknesses in this campaign (stay with Exhibit 2.3):

- The pattern of giving shows strength at the top of the gift chart with the highest level gift already achieved (one gift at $500,000).

- There is a gap at the $250,000 level, which represents the largest percentage of gifts needed.

- While the $10,000 level is strong, there could be more activity initiated below the $10,000 level that might help to fill in some of the dollars needed.

- The campaign is strongest at the lower and middle ranges; that is, gifts from $10,000, $25,000, and $50,000 levels added together represent half of the total raised.

Depending on the nature of the prospect pool, we would recommend the following three strategies for this campaign:

1. *At the top of the gift table:*

- Do not give up on the top gift levels. If there are any prospects who are rated at the $250,000 level or above, intensify the cultivation efforts with them right away.

- Use patience—do not ask for a big gift until the prospect is ready, meaning knowledgeable about your needs.

- If there are no strong prospects at the $250,000+ level, focus on finding two or three more gifts at the $100,000 level to help with this gap, in other words, begin to move down the gift table to fill in holes.

- Consider lengthening the pledge periods for gifts of this size.

- Review recognition policies to make sure the available options at these levels are very attractive to donors.

- Identify a challenge gift at the $100,000 level that could promote the donation of two or three additional gifts at this level.

2. *In the middle of the gift table:*

- Work with the campaign staff to identify 10 to 15 more prospects in the lower and mid-level ranges, where the giving has been strongest, in this case, the $25,000 and $50,000 ranges. This is the new level where the greatest activity should be focused for this campaign. It is entirely possible that more gifts at these ranges will be needed if the $100,000 and $250,000 gift levels remain unmet.

- Identify additional attractive naming and recognition opportunities for these new $25,000 and $50,000 prospects.

- Make this level the next big push with the board and campaign committee. Ask all the leadership volunteers to make their own gifts at this level.

- Focus communication efforts on this level: Use campaign newsletters, materials, and web sites to highlight gifts already made in these ranges.

3. *At the bottom of the gift table:*

- Mount a broader campaign for gifts of $1,000 to $10,000 using volunteer solicitors. At this level it is easier to find prospects, easier to get them to give, and easier to get pledges paid.

- Build excitement for the additional efforts with a new public announcement related to the campaign. This could take the form of a challenge gift, a groundbreaking event, or a special achievement award that will build public awareness of the good work the organization does.

In any campaign there will always be more prospects identified at lower levels than at higher ones. If your campaign is in trouble at the top of the gift table, restructure your plans and activity levels to bring in more donors in the middle and at the bottom levels of giving. Do not forget to keep the top prospects simmering on the back burner; they could be important down the road.

Summary

Fixing a stalled campaign begins with a period of analysis in which you need to determine where the campaign is doing well and where it has faltered. Once these basic fundraising patterns have been identified, you can move forward with finding strategic ways to move the campaign in new directions. Exploring the strengths and weaknesses of your campaign will help lead you to the right methods for putting it back on track.

These are the steps that we recommend for campaign analysis and evaluation:

- Analyze your campaign's fundraising patterns.
- Identify patterns that show strengths or weaknesses in campaign activities.
- Develop a team of campaign fixers selected from across your organization to help create strategies that could set the campaign back on track.

- The strategies you select should first build on strengths that have been established and then attempt to turn weak points into future strengths.

Taking a good look at the holes in your campaign gift table can also be instructive as you target fundraising efforts that will help to jump-start your campaign. Implement more programs and activity that will increase giving at the levels where your campaign is strongest. Build new outreach efforts to attract donors at the middle and lower levels of the gift table when gifts at the top end become harder to close.

More activity is sometimes seen as the best solution for improving gift results, but activity alone will not rebuild a sagging campaign. Take the time to analyze your gift activity, find out what is working and what is not working, and work smarter, not harder. A few months spent strategizing new solutions with your peers can help turn around several years of weak fundraising results.

CHAPTER 3

Identifying Opportunities: Making Lemons out of Lemonade

After reading this chapter you will be able to:

- Improve your stewardship programs to keep donors giving.
- Integrate planned giving into your campaign.
- Build endowment to meet future needs.
- Use new techniques to regain momentum.

Stewardship Is for Keeps

Much advice can be dispensed about how to reach new donors, but the first and most important key to hard times in fundraising is to keep the donors you have.

Why is it important to keep donors? The main reason is that it costs a lot less to go back to known donors than it does to find new ones. Campaign fundraisers usually have to solicit at least three prospects for every gift; with prior donors, that ratio can be improved on dramatically. There are campaigns that bring in gifts from over 70 percent of the prospects solicited! This high ratio of prospects to gifts is produced because these prospects are already well known to the volunteers doing the asking, the prospects already know the organization's case well, and, as prior donors, they already have shown that they care about the cause.

It costs money and time to identify new donors, cultivate them, and solicit them. Even then your efforts will probably only bring in one gift out of three new prospects. Why not spend more time and money where it will be most effective, that is, on prior donors?

Stewardship is the word for all the activities that take place with a donor after a gift has been made. It is instructive to learn what makes donors give to the same organization over and over again. There are a few basic elements of stewardship that apply to almost every campaign. A quick review of these concepts can help you and your colleagues determine if you need to pay attention to this important area (and most of us do). See Exhibit 3.1 to determine your "Stewardship Rating," and prepare to shore up the areas where you scored the weakest.

EXHIBIT 3.1

Determine Your Organization's Stewardship Rating

Rate your organization on a scale of 1 to 3 on each of these stewardship factors, with 3 as the highest rating. Then add up your score and see the chart at the bottom of the exhibit for your own Stewardship Rating.

Campaign Stewardship Activity	1 (Seldom or Never Done)	2 (Done Sometimes)	3 (Always Done)
Thank-you letter out within 48 hours			
Gift receipt out in 48 hours (if done separately from thank-you)			

Quarterly updates sent about campaign progress and needs

Individualized stewardship letters on all gifts over $10,000 (use for 6 to 12 months' follow-up)

Individualized reports on all endowed funds (annually)

Correctly spelled name printed on donor list

Other recognition followed up on within 3 to 6 months (e.g., building signage, special dedications)

Stewardship Rating Results:

Rating of 1 to 10: Watch out—your donors will not stay long.

Rating of 11 to 16: You have room for improvement.

Rating of 17 to 21: You're the best! Your donors love you.

As you can see from the stewardship activities listed in Exhibit 3.1, stewardship is the art of creating a systematic flow of information with current donors about their gifts and the progress of the campaign they gave to. This communication can take many forms depending on the level and type of gift, including: personal letters, calls, e-mails, printed newsletters, e-newsletters, annual reports, and financial statements.

KEY CONCEPT

It costs more to find new donors than it does to keep current donors happy and giving again. Effective stewardship is worth the investment of time and money it takes to keep donors on board.

One key to effective stewardship is to define the types of donor communications that follow each type of gift and set a timetable for their implementation. Try setting a timeframe with your staff for getting gifts processed and thank-you letters out; 48 hours might be an ambitious goal for your organization, but the exercise of meeting deadlines will help your staff to push through logjams that may be slowing thank-you letters down.

Some gifts require personal follow-up within three to six months of the time the donor made the gift. This is a good timetable for contacting capital campaign donors. Let them know the status of the project or facility that is being constructed, review signage, and if possible show them where the site they have named will be located. Hard hat tours are helpful stewardship opportunities at this stage. Use the time with the donors to show them the unfunded areas of the project; with tact, you can also encourage them to up the level of their initial gift to a higher priced, more visible room or naming option.

Donors of endowed funds may prefer to see a financial report on the results of their giving. This can be done annually with a letter from the finance or accounting office that identifies the amount in the corpus of the gift, the earnings, and the income that will be (or has been) spent and what it has been spent on.

Most endowment donors enjoy hearing from a recipient of services that they have funded; for instance, scholarship funders like to hear from scholarship recipients. While this is not a requirement for the institution receiving the gift, an ongoing effort to keep the donor posted on the status of his endowment will usually build the trust and affection of the donor. Since many donors add to their endowed funds over time, their goodwill is useful to the organization.

Not all communication methods used for stewardship purposes must be personalized. Examples of more general materials used in stewardship would be donor lists in annual reports, stories about the ways gifts are used on the web site, and quarterly campaign newsletters. The point here is that a good stewardship plan will include a calendar for what a donor receives, when she receives it, and how often she receives something from your organization after she has made a gift.

Gifts under a certain amount, say $10,000, may require less personalization after the initial thank-you letter and gift receipt goes out. In general, the higher the gift level, the more personal the communication becomes. Some organizations develop personal communication charts for use with top level donors to track calls, mailings, and letters so that they reach maximum effectiveness; too much communication can be annoying, just as too little can leave donors wondering whatever happened to their gift.

Stewardship through Events

Many organizations already do a good job with stewardship through donor events because these kinds of events are popular and known to generate goodwill and publicity. Done well, a strong event can motivate donors to make a second gift. General campaign events can be used for stewardship purposes with all current donors invited, or special invitations can be sent out for unique dedications of certain kinds of gifts.

One good idea is to combine smaller dedications for individual spaces or rooms within the timeframe of a larger dedication during one day or a series of days. This type of stewardship event is organized based on giving levels; in a capital campaign, for instance, the full facility is dedicated at 10 A.M. with a large audience, and the greatest amount of attention is focused on the overall naming donor.

Then, following the full dedication and a short reception, ask other donors to gather with their guests and families for a "flowing dedication." Take a small group of officials through the building, cutting ribbons and thanking donors at each of their spaces. This allows for donors of smaller amounts to be recognized individually and shows appreciation for everyone who made a gift that named a space in the new facility.

The Lifetime Giving Club

Another stewardship idea that is popular in advancement circles, especially in higher education, is the creation of a lifetime donor club. This type of stewardship is for major donors to capital or endowment purposes, not annual fund donors. It is not meant to conflict with annual fund donor clubs, although in setting the rules, you may want to include all annual fund gifts to reach the total.

Universities that create a lifetime giving club usually choose a high dollar level, such as $1 million, that will be meaningful within the context of their donor pool; however, you can select whatever number you think will motivate the donors who give to your organization.

There are several requirements for a lifetime donor club. The gifts must be made from the same entity; bundling family gifts is probably not a good idea unless there is a family foundation that makes the bulk of the gifts. Using matching gifts is probably not appropriate either, since you are promoting consistent support from one individual or giving entity. The highlight of the lifetime giving club is an event that initiates new members into the group, done with all the pomp and circumstance that you can muster.

What is the point of this type of society? Lifetime giving clubs do several things for an institution: First, they honor donors who give large gifts consistently over a period of time, which is the behavior you desire from all donors; second, they are enormously rewarding for the donors themselves, who of course can still keep on giving; and lastly, the entry amount can be used to motivate additional gifts from an individual or giving entity that is close to the total but not quite there yet. Thus the club can be useful for both cultivation of current members and solicitation of members who are near to—or capable of—joining.

 IN THE REAL WORLD

The Donor on the Bicycle

A new science wing was added to the cluster of buildings on a university's main quad. The building was named in honor of a prominent local family foundation, which had given 40 percent of the cost of the project as a naming gift. The campaign goal was reached, the dedication was delightful, and the donors were pleased.

About three months later the VP for avancement got a phone call from the lead trustee of the generous family foundation. He was calling to complain about the lighting on the building. It turned out that he rode his bike around campus in the evenings and could not read his name on the building after dark.

The VP promised to fix it, and her physical plant contacts quickly mounted some artistic spot lights on the building's signage. The donor was happy and this was not the last gift he gave to the institution.

Moral of the story: Do what it takes to keep your donors happy (within reason).

Planned Giving and Your Campaign

Most campaigns do not focus on planned giving tools to help donors meet their needs. This can be a mistake, especially when economic times are bad.

Planned giving is the name given to a set of tools that donors use to make a gift other than with cash or a check. Planned giving usually includes the use of a financial or legal instrument that transfers wealth from the donor to the non-profit. Sometimes, but not always, planned giving can be motivated by the donor's interest in tax savings.

Planned giving can be a helpful option during a period of recession because donors are more cash-strapped during slower economic times than otherwise. Planned gifts are attractive to donors for the following reasons:

- Donors can often make larger gifts with a planned gift option than with cash.

- Donors may be able to realize tax savings for themselves or for their heirs.

- Donors can transfer assets that they are not using at the time of the gift.

- Donors can determine the impact and use of their gifts.

- Donors can provide for their families and for their favorite nonprofits into the future.

Another argument in favor of integrating planned gift options into your campaign, given the current economy, is that it may be worth more to your organization to forego a small gift right now in favor of a larger one later.

EXHIBIT 3.2

Planned Gifts Offer Many Advantages

- Planned gifts allow the donor to make a larger gift than might be possible during his lifetime.

- Planned gifts allow the donor the use of her funds during her lifetime for unforeseeable needs.

- Planned gifts often allow the donor to realize tax advantages.

- Planned gifts can increase retirement income, depending on the vehicle selected.

- Planned gifts can be used to establish an endowed fund to honor a loved one in perpetuity.

- Planned gifts can allow the donor to pass assets to his heirs at a lower transfer tax cost.

Some organizations are afraid to ask for planned gifts because they think it will take away from current campaign gifts that are more expendable, and therefore, more desirable. Although it is true that most planned gifts employ long-term giving strategies, not all of them fit this definition. As you can see from Exhibit 3.2, planned gifts can offer many advantages to donors and to your organization.

Not all planned gifts are for the longer term. Some planned gifts that can bring immediate assets to the nonprofit include:

- Gifts of personal property, such as gems or art (if they can be sold).

- Gifts of real estate (must be sold).

- Gifts of publicly traded securities (stocks and bonds).

- Charitable lead trusts.

- Gifts of retirement income or IRAs.

It is important to remember that those representing the nonprofit should not attempt to give financial advice to the prospect. Be sure to train all volunteers and staff who might be working in your campaign to tell donors to check

---

EXHIBIT 3.3

Types of Planned Gifts

- Securities
- Life insurance
- Bequests
- Charitable remainder trusts
- Charitable gift annuities
- Charitable lead trusts
- Gifts of retirement plans and IRAs
- Gifts of real estate or personal property

---

with their accountant, attorney, or financial advisor as they consider making a planned gift.

The role of the campaign staff member or campaign volunteer is to be aware of the kinds of planned gifts the institution offers, to be ready to discuss these kinds of gifts with the donor, and to bring them up if the prospect offers an opening for this discussion (see Exhibit 3.3). There is nothing wrong with the volunteer bringing up the subject if he or she is clear about not providing financial or legal advice to the donor.

Bequests

Giving through a bequest is a very attractive planned giving tool for both donors and nonprofits. For donors, giving through a bequest can be one part of a larger plan to distribute their assets to family and favored charities. For nonprofits, bequests represent some of their largest gifts, and often come unannounced, with little fanfare or donor cultivation required. It can be rewarding, however, to find ways to market bequests to your donor group. (See Exhibit 3.4.)

Only 48 percent, or less than half, of all Americans have a will (from a 2007 study on bequests from the Center on Philanthropy at Indiana

University). This is woefully low, and shows that there is still a need to remind your constituents about the value of planning where their assets will go after their death. It can be a difficult subject, but there are some tried and true ways to market bequests.

TIPS AND TECHNIQUES

An Approach to Starting the Conversation with a Donor about a Bequest

- You have a great relationship with our organization.
- What is it that we do that you value?
- What are your concerns about our organization over the longer term, let us say 10 to 20 years from now?
- Would you be willing to explore some ways to help us deal with those concerns?
- We would like you to consider making a gift that could help our organization meet those goals, perhaps as a part of your estate planning.

Planned giving materials are best aimed at the 55+ age group, although recent research has shown that people in their 40s and early 50s are already writing their wills. Planned giving professionals will tell you that other important indicators (besides age) for planned giving prospects include donors who have made consistent gifts over time (no matter how small); donors who have no children; and donors who are undergoing major financial changes, such as the sale of a private company.

EXHIBIT 3.4

How to Market Bequests and Other Planned Gifts

- Create a planned giving committee; put lawyers, financial advisors, and accountants on it. Use them to give you advice and review materials.

- Create a planned gift brochure, which outlines types of gifts and your organization's policies, and gives contact information for follow-up.

- Use your direct mailing list to mine for planned giving prospects. Consider using a service that will identify the age of your donors if you do not collect that information.

- Develop a planned giving recognition society. Give it a name (e.g., the Heritage Society), an identity, an event, and recognition. List bequest society members prominently in your materials. (Make sure that donors agree to have their name listed!)

- Develop a quarterly or semiannual planned giving newsletter. Use it to feature changes in IRS rules or Congressional actions about gifts, to feature a planned giving donor, to explain one or more giving vehicles, and to advertise the planned giving society.

- Train your campaign volunteers, staff members, and executive director/ CEO in basic planned giving tools to give them information and confidence with donors.

- Create a policy on how to count planned gifts and how to recognize them within your campaign. Don't forget that bequests are not irrevocable! Be cautious in what you promise, as donors can—and do—change their minds and their wills.

As in any other fundraising effort, personal relationships are important in asking for and closing planned gifts. Take the time to listen to the donor and see what type of gift meets her needs best. Ask if you can talk to her financial advisor, if that seems useful.

Stewardship, or keeping in touch with the donor beyond the actual writing of the bequest, is a key element of planned giving because bequests are not irrevocable. We have seen donors change their minds years after making a will that includes their favorite charities. Small insults can loom large in the minds of some older donors who believe they should be treated like major donors, even if the money is still in their hands. The best advice is to treat bequest donors with respect and keep them focused on the good work of your organization.

Keep the donor advised of any changes in your organization's policies regarding planned gifts or changes instituted by the IRS or by Congress. Do not rush things; in the planned giving world, it takes time to get the right gift for the right donor, but the result can be worth a great deal to the institution. Finally, do your best to represent the long-term interests of the organization. It is not fair (or ethical) to bait and switch a donor and gain a small gift for the current campaign if a larger bequest could be solidified down the road. Both the donor and the nonprofit will be rewarded if you succeed.

TIPS AND TECHNIQUES

Types of Bequests

Bequests can be made in any of the following ways:

- The donor can name a specific dollar amount that goes to the charity.
- The gift can be a percentage of the total estate.
- The gift can be residual, that is, whatever is left after everything else has been given out.
- The gift can be made with a specific asset such as stock, bonds, gems, real estate, or a work of art.
- The gift can be a contingent bequest in which the recipient organization has to meet some requirement before it gets the money.
- The gift can be unrestricted or restricted to any purpose the donor feels is appropriate. If the organization cannot meet (or does not wish to meet) the requirements of the donor, it is free to not accept the gift.

Planned giving will not take the place of gifts of cash and pledges needed in your campaign, but it is one tool that can help build long-term support for your needs from donors whose current assets are substantially downgraded. (See Exhibit 3.5.) Do not take no for an answer when a donor clearly wants to help your organization succeed; bring out a full array of planned giving vehicles that might help close the gift.

EXHIBIT 3.5

Charitable Lead Trusts

The charitable lead trust is a planned giving vehicle that allows the donor to make a gift to the nonprofit while passing on assets to heirs at a lower transfer tax cost. A lead trust pays either fixed or variable income to the nonprofit, depending on the type of trust selected, usually over a number of years.

When the trust term ends, the principal goes to the donor's family (or other designated heirs). When properly established and funded, the trust can be a vehicle for reducing gift and estate taxes. If grandchildren will ultimately receive the trust assets, careful planning can help to minimize or eliminate the generation-skipping transfer tax.

The creation of a charitable lead trust can help the donor to meet three goals:

1. The creation of a charitable lead trust could help the donor with estate planning by removing key assets from the estate and passing them to heirs with potential tax advantages to the donor and to them.

2. The income created from the lead trust would flow to the nonprofit organization for an established number of years, and could be directed to support construction, endowment, operations, or other high-priority needs as designated by the donor.

3. A leadership gift derived from a charitable lead trust could be recognized appropriately by the nonprofit through a high-level recognition or naming opportunity, since the trust will produce a reliable income stream for the institution that can be aggregated over a period of time for recognition purposes.

Note: This type of trust is highly complex and requires skilled legal and financial advice. While you can suggest that a donor look into this option, do not attempt to provide specific advice on how to implement the gift vehicle.

An Opportunity to Build for the Future

Fundraising in difficult times is not all about reducing goals, staff layoffs, and raising smaller gifts. Truly farsighted nonprofit leaders will look at this time as an opportunity to reposition their organizations for future growth. Now that you are familiar with planned giving as a campaign tool, link planned gifts with gifts to the endowment. Both planned giving and endowment giving provide long-term support for the organization and its needs.

Think Endowment

Capital campaigns are all about growth, and this is a period where growth potential may be seen as limited. More shiny new buildings and polished marble floors may suddenly look like excessive spending at a time when companies and individuals are cutting back. Luxury is out of fashion, and so is taking on more debt. Use this period to find ways to build for the long term. In fundraising terms, building for the long term always means endowment.

Endowment campaigns (or endowment components of current campaigns) have a special flavor. They can move more slowly than capital campaigns, since building endowment is a long-term goal. They can employ planned giving strategies, since the very largest endowment gifts are often made through trusts and bequests. And they focus on the future health of the organization, which works well in a time when short-term fundraising may present special difficulties.

Add Endowment as a Component to Your Ongoing Campaign

One way to jump-start your current campaign is to restructure your published needs and create an endowment component for your campaign. This component can either take the place of needs that you are willing to put on the back burner, or it can be added on to a campaign goal that already exists. In this latter case, you may want to use the addition of the endowment component to add time to the campaign.

Endowed gifts are those gifts where the principal is maintained and invested by the institution, but the interest and/or income is spent on an annual basis according to a policy set by the organization. Most nonprofits, up until the recent market decline, have been spending about 4 to 5 percent of their endowment income per year. The income must be spent on the area or program designated by the donor, which requires some bookkeeping on the part of the recipient organization.

Only the donor can create a true endowment. If the board or administration of a nonprofit decides to treat a large gift as an endowment, that's fine, but a different board or administration can change that decision. Endowments are protected legally from incursion (except in times of financial exigency). Heirs can and will litigate whether the institution has proceeded correctly with the expenditures from an endowed fund if the endowment is spent on other areas than those designated in the original gift agreement.

Adding an endowment component to your campaign may seem counterintuitive, but it has its attractions. There are several reasons why this move could be a positive one for your board: Raising endowment emphasizes long-term fiscal responsibility; it creates a new giving area to attract donors who are "endowment friendly"; and it provides a new incentive to refresh the campaign, perhaps also providing a new timetable.

Gifts of endowment are attractive to certain kinds of donors. In general, the larger national foundations are not too eager to make endowed gifts, because they already operate like an endowment. Foundations make gifts of 5 percent per year out of income that is earned off of assets. Their principal remains invested, just like most endowments at nonprofit organizations. Family foundations, however, do have an interest in seeing to the long-term health of organizations that they support, and they can often prove to be good potential prospects for endowed gifts.

Individuals are probably the best endowment gift candidates. Look for older members of your prospect pool, since endowment gifts are often developed using a planned giving tool, such as a bequest or trust. Consider your more financially sophisticated prospects as endowment candidates, since endowment giving requires some concept of long-term investments, dividends, and payouts.

Do not forget that endowment donors also enjoy recognition! There are several ways to provide recognition for donors of endowed gifts. Note that the recognition does not have to follow the money exactly. For instance, if the donor gives $100,000 to endow a program, as long as you spend the money the way the donor designates it, you can still name a room or a space to recognize the gift.

Set a policy for a minimum level endowed gift that can be used to create a separate, named endowed fund for accounting and recognition purposes. Many organizations select a dollar value, such as $10,000, $25,000, or even higher, for this purpose. The problem with lower level endowed gifts is that the effort of investing, tracking, and accounting the gift and then allocating it for the designated purpose may be greater than the annual payout is worth to the organization.

TIPS AND TECHNIQUES

Here Are Some Ideas for Recognition of Endowment Donors

- Name endowed chairs for staff or faculty whose salary is underwritten with an endowed fund.
- Create named funds in the library to honor endowed gifts.
- Name scholarships or financial aid for donors.
- Name a program that is endowed by the donor, and give her credit at events that feature this program.
- Name a department, a whole school, or an entire campus for a large endowed gift.
- Name rooms or spaces on your site, just as with a capital donor, for a specific level of endowed gift.
- Put names of all endowment donors on a permanent plaque.
- Write about an endowment donor in your publications and on your web site.
- Include endowment donors in your campaign recognition plans.
- Hold an event or reception to thank all endowment donors.

Enhancement versus Budget Relief

There is a difference you need to be aware of between raising endowment for enhancement and raising endowment for budget relief (that is, paying for things already in the budget).

In the case of enhancement, the endowment is being raised to create new programs. For instance, imagine that your organization wants to expand to provide services in a new region. You might want to approach a donor to ask for an endowment to continue the work over a period of years, rather than just starting it and stopping it as money becomes available. In other words, the endowment provides continuity, but for a program that is new. This kind of endowment works well for the philanthropist who is entrepreneurial and wants to see some impact from his gift.

Endowment for budget relief, on the other hand, is a fiscally conservative measure that provides ongoing budget support for programs that are already in the operating budget of the organization. This is the kind of endowment that universities build, because it provides support on an annual basis for operational costs such as financial aid, salaries, and maintenance. Endowment for budget relief requires more discipline to raise, because instead of building fancy new programs, the gift supports the long-term fiscal health of the institution.

Asking for endowment for budget relief is probably going to be more successful with those who are close to the organization and who have a personal interest in seeing it succeed over the long term. The best prospects for this kind of endowment are also your very best donors: current board members, past board members, graduates, prior patients, and families who have experienced or place special value on the services your organization provides.

Be careful about how you count endowment in your campaign. If planned gifts are a major focus of the endowment portion of the campaign, you probably do not want to count bequests and trusts at face value. Bequests are not irrevocable, and the donor who is excited about endowing your organization today may not be there for you tomorrow.

A wise precaution is to carry planned gift totals as a separate column in your campaign totals, so that the board can see the difference between gifts of cash and pledges and gifts that are longer term. You may wish to set a separate or ancillary campaign goal for long-term gifts, or some similar nomenclature, that is over and above the goal for cash and pledges. Place a discounted value on long-term gifts if this is appropriate in your environment, but do not plan to spend the money until it is realized!

IN THE REAL WORLD

The Endowment that Keeps on Giving

The head of a family foundation created an endowment to help students attend a private institution of higher education. Like many such gifts, the endowed fund was named in honor of the donor's parents. The initial gift was for $25,000, which was the minimum endowment gift level required to set up a separate, named fund.

After the untimely death of the original donor, his children and other family members made memorial gifts to the original endowed fund. The institution went on to ask for additional gifts from the family foundation, which continued to grow the fund. Within 10 years the fund had exceeded $1 million through a combination of growth in the original investments, additional foundation gifts, and memorial gifts. Thus the donor's original intent, to provide financial support for needy students and to honor his parents, was not only met but surpassed.

Techniques to Restore Campaign Momentum

Momentum is a key ingredient in all successful campaigns. All campaigns build momentum through the accrual of major gifts, the setting of a timeframe, and the movement forward toward reaching a goal. The best campaigns have a snowball effect, in which early gifts build excitement because they are large, and they in turn inspire later gifts from smaller donors to reach the goal. The unique combination of enhanced fundraising activity, increased PR, and outreach to new constituencies tends to build into an outpouring of support for the campaign and the organization. In fact, it is exactly this ability to increase and enhance the visibility of the nonprofit that leads many groups to mount a campaign to begin with.

The problem with a stalled campaign is that forward momentum has declined or even stopped. The urge to join with others to meet specified needs has been staunched, either by mistakes made in the campaign itself, or by the stultifying effect of the economic downturn on fundraising in general. What can you do to restore momentum once it is lost? We will discuss several alternatives for building momentum back up in this section that might work for your campaign.

Using Challenges and Matches in Your Campaign

One popular element used to restore campaign momentum is a method borrowed from the annual fund campaign. The effective use of challenges and matches can help to jumpstart a stalled campaign by giving it new life and renewed excitement. Here are some examples of how challenges and matches can be used in an ongoing campaign:

- *Create a Leadership Challenge.* Go back to your major campaign donors and ask them to make a new gift toward a set goal for a Leadership Challenge Fund, such as $1 million. Once the $1 million Challenge Fund is in place, use it as a challenge match to attract new donors to the campaign. The challenge can be made on a 2:1 basis, that is, for every new donor who gives $100,000 the campaign will match the gift with $50,000 from the Leadership Challenge Fund. This gives your campaign the potential to raise a new $3 million ($1 million from the Leadership Challenge Fund plus $2 million more from the new donors).

- *Ask all current donors to add one extra year to their campaign pledges at the same level of funding.* For a campaign with five-year pledges, this will add 20 percent to the campaign total in one fell swoop.

- *Find a foundation that will match gifts (up to a certain amount) from new donors to your organization on a 1:1 basis.* For instance, the Kresge Foundation has been generously supporting capital campaigns for years with matching gifts of this type. This is a great way to build momentum in the public phase of the campaign.

- *Pick five cities or geographic areas that are important to your organization.* Build a campaign committee of volunteers in each city. Then develop a challenge between the cities as a competition to see who can raise the most money for a specific purpose. Consider, for instance, creating "The New York City Scholarship Fund," an endowed fund used to support students from New York, or something similar that fits your campaign needs. (Note: this concept also works as a competition among reunion classes at schools and colleges.)

Donors love leveraging their gifts, and the concept of leveraging dollars can work with small donors or large donors. Work with your board or campaign committee to see what size and style of challenge will appeal to your constituents.

Use PR and Events to Create Campaign Momentum

Another way to build momentum in a campaign is to use events and PR more strategically in support of campaign needs and timing. Because they come from different backgrounds and have different priorities, PR and advancement professionals do not always agree on how to put together a strong outreach effort. Here are some ideas that can help to bridge that gap between fundraising and public relations.

1. *Mount a regional PR effort to show off the organization and its needs.* Pick a theme that supports the campaign. Create a buzz around this theme with public events, ads, an e-mail blast, and contests. This type of publicity effort works best in the public phase of the campaign, when outreach to new audiences is a key to success.

2. *Create a list of target cities where you have identified key prospects.* Share the list with your PR folks and get them to help you brainstorm about how to make your organization more visible in those target areas.

3. *Plan a series of smaller campaign kick off events rather than one large one.* Use the events to target specific prospect groups, such as corporate donors, foundation trustees, or first-time donors. Focus volunteer efforts on getting the right audience to each event.

4. *Take your campaign on the road.* If your campaign has stalled at home, and if you have a regional or national donor pool, take your campaign out of town. Your programs and services will attract new attention from a fresh audience. Take the time to meet supporters ahead of an out of town event and set up local host committees to attract the audience you desire.

5. *Ask for donated billboards.* In the current economy, advertisers are cutting back, and billboard space may be available at a discount or for free. Investigate other advertising that might be donated, such as newspaper and magazine ads, talk radio, public service announcements, and banners on popular local Internet news sites.

6. *Create a sense of exclusivity for your donors.* Find new ways to make donating to your campaign a sign of prestige in your community. Create a new benefits program for top donor categories. Add travel opportunities and offer special trips that are limited to donors of $5,000+, for instance. Or hold small group dinners at exclusive homes (where the hosts pay) and only invite $10,000+ donors and prospects.

Rebuild Momentum through Sight-Raising Techniques

Sight-raising is the use of various techniques to encourage higher level giving among a group of prospects and donors who interact with each other. Sight-raising is commonly used in campaigns during the silent phase, especially to motivate higher level giving from boards and campaign committees. However, sight-raising techniques can be adopted by campaigns that have slowed down to try and raise the gift levels. Closing larger gifts from more donors will help re-build the momentum of the campaign, so sight-raising can be an effective tool to jump-start campaigns that are slowing down.

KEY CONCEPT

Sight-raising with prospects and donors can help to close higher level gifts, bringing you closer to reaching your campaign goal.

Sight-raising techniques start with the internal groups most likely to be sup-porters of the campaign, that is, boards, advisory councils, and committees. The idea is to set an expectation that the members of these groups will give larger dollar amounts than they have in the past. This is done by selecting a target gift amount—say, $25,000. The gift amount has to be carefully chosen, because it should be a little higher than past gifts from the group of donors you are work-ing with, but within the capability of most of the members of the group.

Once the target gift amount is settled, then concentrate attention on this gift amount and the levels above it in all campaign communications, including board reports, printed materials, recognition programs, campaign newsletters, web site announcements, and so on. If new gifts are announced or featured, limit them to the $25,000 level or higher.

The repetition of a specific gift level needs to be reinforced by producing several gifts closed at that level. Identify one or two core donors in your organi-zation's inner circle whom you can count on to make a $25,000 gift. Use these gifts to set the bar for others. In other words, once the gift level expected of a board member is seen to be $25,000 or more, other board members will follow suit. The combination of peer pressure and expectation from the organization's closest friends helps to keep the dollar figure at the level you have selected.

IN THE REAL WORLD

Sight-Raise with Donor Recognition

One way to encourage sight-raising is to raise the entry level for basic donor recognition. A museum had engraved the names of all its donors of $10,000 or more on its donor wall in the entrance lobby. To encourage sight-raising at the beginning of a new phase of its capital campaign, the museum created a new donor wall outside that required a minimum gift of $25,000. Not surprisingly, its campaign donors were suddenly giving $25,000 instead of $10,000!

The pricing structure for various campaign recognition options can also be adjusted to help with sight-raising. Recognition pricing is very important, especially in a capital campaign, where "buying" a room or space is usually an attraction to the donor.

Consider the top end of the recognition table, which is usually the exterior naming of the building or facility. Make sure that your top gift is as high as you can possibly ask for, because that one gift will make up for a lot of smaller gifts lower on the gift table. For instance, exterior naming options are often set at 30 percent to 40 percent of the cost of the project. Consider asking for up to 50 percent of the cost in the naming gift if you have a prospect with the capability to make a commitment at that level.

Another technique for closing a larger gift is to increase the goal of the campaign so that any set percentage of the campaign total is a larger number. Increase a capital campaign goal by adding an endowment portion, perhaps a maintenance endowment, thus adding 20 percent to the overall goal of the campaign. (Building and operations endowments are generally viewed as fiscally responsible by most boards, so your board will most likely approve this move.) Thus, your campaign goal will increase by 20 percent from, say, $4 million to $5 million. Then set the exterior naming price at 50 percent of the new amount, or $2.5 million. In this manner, by raising the goal to meet future needs, you also can raise the price of key naming options.

Sight-raising can also be a factor in defining the low end of the recognition table. Let us say that you are building an educational wing that has 10 classrooms. Your campaign committee suggests they be priced at $25,000 each, an accessible number for many donors. Consider instead raising the individual classroom price to $30,000 or $35,000; when amortized over 5-year pledges, the extra amount is only $1,000 to $2,000 more a year per donor, but the total net to your campaign is significant (10 classrooms × $25,000 = $250,000; 10 classrooms × $35,000 = $350,000, or almost 30 percent more.)

TIPS AND TECHNIQUES

Ideas for Sight-Raising with Your Donors

❶ *Ask for a certain percentage of the campaign in one gift.* Set the top level gift as a percentage of your campaign, perhaps as much as 20 to 25 percent of the goal. Talk about the amount and ask your volunteers to help you find that donor.

❷ *Cluster gifts around one new, higher level.* Identify a higher gift level that you think a small group of high-end donors close to your organization could reach. Then ask one or two of them to make a gift at that level and use the announcement of those new gifts to set an expectation for the others.

❸ *Start donor recognition at a higher dollar amount.* Set a new, higher level of giving for names to go on your donor wall or for naming spaces in a new building.

❹ *Focus announcements about new gifts on a specific level of giving.* Choose a minimum gift level and only make public announcements about gifts at this level or above, even in oral reports to boards and committees.

Summary

Your campaign can be strengthened by adding new elements and new giving tools to the fundraising mix. To begin with, focus on donor stewardship to keep current donors informed and happy with the organization. Keeping current donors giving is the most cost-effective way to find prospects for your campaign.

Planned giving offers a set of tools that you and your volunteers can use to gain support for your organization's needs both for the short term and longer term. Training volunteers and staff in planned giving techniques will allow them to approach donors with different kinds of giving vehicles in a period when current assets may be difficult to tap. Adding gifts to the endowment as a component of campaign giving can also provide a strong link with planned gifts, since both endowed gifts and planned gifts are mainly concerned with providing support far into the future for the organization.

There are numerous techniques that can be used to provide momentum in a campaign that has slowed down. Matches and campaign challenges can provide excitement, and they usually prove to be useful in attracting new donors, along with helping to secure a second gift from current donors.

Providing more PR support and creating a series of events to take out on the road to target new audiences are two additional ideas for building momentum after the campaign has slowed down. Sight-raising techniques are also important when large gifts are needed to energize a campaign that is lagging.

CHAPTER 4

Get Back on Track with Changes in Campaign Structure

After reading this chapter, you will be able to:

- Adjust campaign phasing and timetables.
- Manage campaign goals and gift tables.
- Select pricing and recognition levels that work for your campaign.

Campaign Phasing and Timetables

The details of campaign phasing and timing provide a more sensitive structural framework than many fundraising professionals realize. One of the key components that separates capital campaign fundraising from general major gift work is that campaigns are set up with timed segments, known as phases, and an overall timeframe within which to meet the goal. It is this very aspect of timing that gives campaigns their momentum and builds their sense of urgency. Without timing and phasing, the campaign is just a big wish list of organizational needs.

What if your campaign is behind its original timetable and goals? Given the difficult external environment, pushing the timetable back is definitely a choice that you should be considering. While adding six months or a year to a campaign should not be a knee-jerk reaction, it does allow several factors to come into play. Adding time to the campaign gives the organization several additional options:

- Adding time allows the advancement staff more time to identify new donors.

- It gives new donors more time to be cultivated and become engaged in the work of the nonprofit.

- It allows prospects who have already been solicited time to consider their financial resources before making a commitment.

- It could allow pledge periods to be lengthened, which might cut the number of unpaid campaign pledges going forward. It is usually better for the organization if goals can be met, even if it takes longer, rather than not meeting goals at all.

There are some risks to expanding the timetable that need to be factored into your decision-making. First, if construction is already under way in a building being funded by the capital campaign, the project may require a certain level of cash flow on a quarterly or annual basis. Interfering with or stopping construction can be costly and can bring permanent damage to the reputation of your nonprofit.

Second, as many experienced campaign professionals can attest, campaigns run on momentum. Building urgency around the needs of the organization is a motivational tool to help donors reach a decision and close a gift. Without the sense of urgency and immediate need that keeps a campaign going, it is easy for volunteers and donors to lose focus. Keeping a tight timetable puts pressure on everyone—staff, volunteers, and prospects—and that pressure creates the high level of energy and enthusiasm that translates into gifts. Letting the pressure out—by lengthening the timeline—could have the effect of letting the campaign sag, or lose momentum, at a critical juncture.

When Changing the Campaign's Timeline

❶ Establish a range for the timetable instead of a fixed number of months or years:

- Say the campaign will take from 18 months to 2 years.
- Use the timeline to allow some flexibility with volunteers and donors.

❷ Assess the internal requirements for making the campaign succeed and add the amount of time necessary to complete those tasks:

- If new prospects must be identified, cultivated and solicited, that process can take from 12 to 18 months.
- If new volunteers need to be trained and engaged, only 3 to 6 months might be required.

❸ Start with a smaller time increment, perhaps 6 months to a year:

- Leave the door open to add more time if it becomes necessary.
- Jumping to add 2 or 3 more years at once could hurt the sense of urgency around your needs.

❹ Keep an eye on the external environment:

- If economic conditions begin to ease up, move ahead faster.
- Study the fundraising results of peer organizations.
- Keep up with giving trends in your community.

❺ Understand the specific nature of your prospect pool:

- Focus earlier on prospects whose businesses are more recession-proof.
- If most of your prospects have experienced substantial business losses, add more time to let them get back on their feet.
- If your top prospects have experienced a large decline in assets or ability to give, push the timeline back. You will need to replace their gifts, augment their gifts (if the gifts come in smaller), or wait for them to recover.

Adjusting Campaign Phases

It may be easier to adjust the timeline for phases of the campaign than it would be to move the overall campaign timeline back. The most common use of phases is to help distinguish the early, silent phase of the campaign from the later, public phase of the drive.

Before making any changes, consider the purposes behind having a silent phase to begin with. These purposes include:

- Closing gifts from those prospects who are closest to the organization, including board members, campaign volunteers, and past supporters.

- Raising a significant portion of the goal to give confidence that the campaign can reach its total goal.

- Testing specific goals and needs to see if donors will support them.

- Closing gifts at the top end of the gift table to secure the large level gifts that will make the campaign numbers work.

Given the uncertainties of the economic conditions we face, meeting all of these objectives may simply take more time than was originally planned, even with the best planning and staffing available. It is much smarter to extend the silent phase and meet all the goals identified than to rush into the public phase of the campaign. Entering the public phase too early means that you run the risk of announcing the goal and then finding that either the resources at the top of the gift table are not available or the needs identified are not striking a sympathetic chord with your donors. In either case, it is far more embarrassing to back down on a goal after the public phase has commenced than to adjust it during the silent phase.

Phasing Based on Type of Giving

Not all campaigns utilize the basic two-phase structure of a silent phase followed by a public phase. Other options for a campaign that shows signs of slowing down include changing the sequence of phases, dropping some of the phases, and/or separating out specific needs. Separate needs can then be translated into sequential phases, each with its own mini-goal and mini-timeline.

For instance, a campaign that has been fundraising for endowment and capital gifts together in one drive could change to conduct two sequential campaigns. Thus the campaign would meet its needs one at a time, rather than pushing for both at once. While running two campaigns sequentially will take longer than combining both needs into one drive, the ability to reach success in both areas over the long term will have a more beneficial effect on the organization than trying to do both simultaneously and falling short on both.

Remember that any changes in phasing or timing need to be integrated with the timing and execution of the internal plans to implement new programs or facilities funded by the campaign. It takes a combination of restructured phasing and goals, revised program plans, and flexibility in fundraising to create a new and powerful plan as the organization moves forward to meet new realities.

 IN THE REAL WORLD

A capital campaign to build a new facility at a community health organization started out with a bang. Key supporters in the community coalesced around the need for a new building, and gifts from individuals, corporations, and foundations poured in. The silent phase had just reached $11 million toward the $18 million goal when the fundraising suddenly hit a wall.

A quick analysis of the campaign results showed that most of the prospects identified and rated as capable of making gifts of $25,000 or more had already made their gifts.

The organization's leadership moved quickly to make changes. First, they declared a six-month time-out from the campaign to reassess their needs for the building. Their planning was conducted on three different levels: 1) they conducted a long-term strategic planning exercise with their board to confirm their future needs; 2) they conducted an analysis of potential revenue opportunities to make sure that they had the funds to operate their new facility; and 3) they hired a fundraising consultant to identify new markets for their fundraising programs.

(Continued)

At the end of the six-month planning period, the organization was ready to move ahead. The leadership team had made changes in two basic areas: First, they cut back on the size of the new facility to meet the operational budget level they projected they were able to support.

Second, on the fundraising front, the campaign moved immediately into its public phase so that it could tap into a broader potential donor base. The organization focused on two lower-level fundraising programs to meet the rest of its capital needs. The first program was the addition of a new donor society for gifts of $1,000 to $10,000. The campaign also added a new viral internal component, complete with an interactive web site, to develop and broaden its donor base below the $1,000 level.

In addition, the timetable for the campaign was extended from two to three years. With these changes in hand, the campaign was able to rebuild its momentum and move rapidly toward its new, lower goal.

There are several steps to changing the timeline of a campaign. If you take them in this order, you will be ready to start again with new strategies in hand after a brief time-out:

1. Take a campaign time-out to analyze the results to date.

2. Conduct long-term planning to readjust program needs, goals, and costs to meet new realities.

3. Shift the strategy and timing of the fundraising program:

　a. By moving faster into the public phase of the campaign.

　b. By creating two new lower-level fundraising programs.

　c. By adding one more year to the overall timeline.

KEY CONCEPT

Establish the timetable of your campaign within a range, say, of two to three years, instead of announcing a fixed timetable to allow for flexibility as donors react to the economic environment.

Learn to Adjust Campaign Goals and Gift Tables

It is important to understand that ultimately, the capability to reach specified goals within a set timeframe in a campaign depends on the actions of *donors*, not on the actions of staff or volunteers. Staff and volunteers can strategize and implement new programs, and surely their actions do influence donors in many ways, but the power remains at the donor end of the relationship. Therefore one must understand that as the behavior of donors changes to accommodate new economic realities, the behavior of staff and volunteers must change, too. To continue doing everything as it has been done in the past will ensure failure.

In many ways, uncertainty in the markets and the resulting loss of confidence are bigger enemies to a fundraising campaign than the actual loss of financial assets. A sophisticated donor can adjust to having fewer assets available and yet still make a giving decision based on her overall financial picture. The same donor, faced with the uncertainties of an economy moving into recession, will simply hedge her bets and wait it out to see how her finances perform before committing to a large philanthropic contribution. This donor holding pattern can hurt your campaign.

KEY CONCEPT

The time it takes for a donor to make his decision about a gift increases proportionately with the level of uncertainty in the economy.

Raise More in the Silent Phase

What does this uncertainty mean for your campaign's goals? Do not automatically assume that the best thing to do immediately is to lower the goal. Think first about ways to increase the participation and gift levels of those who are nearest to the organization and who already recognize the urgency of your needs. Start with the silent phase of the campaign, when donors who are closest usually make their initial gifts.

In times of economic distress, it is wise to use the silent phase to raise an even higher percentage of the goal than would be recommended in a normal economy. Instead of looking for 50 percent to 60 percent of the total funds needed before going public, consider extending the silent phase to raise as much as 70 percent to 80 percent of the total goal. Then extend the timetable for the silent phase to allow the new, higher goal to be reached.

The reason for setting the silent phase goal higher is to give the campaign additional credibility and stability in a time of uncertainty. Going public with 70 percent or 75 percent of the total goal in hand gives potential donors much more assurance that the organization remains strong and that the campaign will succeed in meeting its goals.

Break Up the Goals

It is very important to avoid either the reality or the appearance of failure in a capital campaign. Failure can be destructive to the public image of the organization, and could impede gifts for years to come. We recommend going to great lengths to preserve the appearance of success in reaching campaign goals, even if "success" means biting off a smaller amount to chew. Nonprofits in trouble have something in common with the recent banking crisis: If public trust in a nonprofit institution is destroyed, it is like a run on a bank, the lack of trust will destroy the organization very quickly.

Given the need to keep the organization's reputation strong, think about various options to restructure campaign goals so that some goals can be met. One option for changing goals in a difficult environment is to break out the components of the overall goal and focus on fundraising for one component at a time.

Imagine that an $8 million campaign was originally planned to raise $5 million for a new building and $3 million to renovate an old building. Break up the two projects and start with the renovation, which appears to be a more conservative choice. While raising the $3 million for the renovation first is more feasible, it will also show your donors that you are responding to the external environment. Starting smaller will allow you to assess the potential for additional support without going too far out on a limb, financially speaking.

After the first phase is completed, then extend the campaign to the second phase, which will focus on the $5 million for the new construction. Rent additional space if necessary while Phase 2 is being completed. It is preferable to extend a rental period than to start a construction project and not have enough cash on hand to finish it.

KEY CONCEPT

At a time when your donors are taking action to cut or pull back in their business and financial activities, show them that you, too, have planned conservatively in order to earn their philanthropic support.

There may come a time when it becomes necessary to cut or modify the overall campaign goals. In addition to expanding the timeline and breaking up goals, you may want to employ one the following methods for changing your campaign goal.

Delay Endowment Goals

The purpose of the goal is to identify a finishing point, so that campaign donors and volunteers know that the needs as identified are met, and the organization can move ahead with the programs and facilities that it requires. The goals identified can be short-term or long-term, however, especially when endowment is added to the mix.

In tough times, consider delaying the endowment phase of your campaign. For now, immediate cash and pledges are more likely to be required to keep current operations going. Raising gifts for the endowment—a long-term institutional goal—may have to take a back seat to meeting more immediate needs for space, operations, and programs. Endowment campaigns can be structured to take advantage of planned gifts, or they can be delayed and put into a separate campaign phase.

Integrate the Annual Fund with the Campaign

Another standard component of the overall advancement program that can be adjusted as circumstances warrant is the inclusion or exclusion of the annual fund (funds raised for annual operational expenses) in the overall campaign goal.

Some organizations prefer to run comprehensive campaigns, where capital and program needs are added to the annual fund goal to create one large campaign effort. The comprehensive approach generally incurs positive benefits for the annual fund by keeping it in front of donors, including it in campaign asks, and bringing the full weight of the campaign structure to bear in support of operational needs.

If your campaign does not include the annual fund in its campaign goals, consider making a change to include the annual fund and its goal in the overall campaign goal. (Multiply the annual fund goal times the number of years for a multiyear campaign.) It is also possible to add in the annual fund goal, but then to take out the same amount in other identified needs, thus bringing the total campaign goal back to the same level it was without the annual fund goal.

While this change may seem like robbing Peter to pay Paul—and it will have ramifications within the organization—the switch allows for two important things to happen: The annual fund becomes part of the campaign's priorities, which gives more attention to raising money for current needs; and the overall goal remains the same, precluding a sense of failure among key external constituencies. In other words, it changes fundraising priorities to focus on cash flow, while lowering the "new money" goal and preserving face in the community.

Cut the Goal Outright

Some organizations will make the decision to cut their campaign goals outright. If this happens in your organization, be sure that the internal planning phase comes first, as the new lower goals must match reduced needs inside the organization.

Cutting back on new programs or new facilities—or simply delaying them—is an honorable and appropriate response to challenging economic circumstances. Remember, however, that the decision making process becomes important as cuts are made. Explain clearly to all involved, whether inside or outside the organization, how the decisions were made and on what basis programs were cut or delayed.

Financial transparency is even more important in tough times than when things are going well, because decisions that are important to the future of the organization are being made, often quickly. Try to avoid internal or board battles over scare resources—these fights can get ugly, and they waste valuable time and effort. Follow the best examples of crisis leadership: Consider all the input that is available, make decisions quickly, do not waffle, present the decisions as pragmatic and finally, do not get defensive, and move on.

Identify Additional Sources of Revenue

A final idea about reducing goals is to identify other sources of income that could be tapped to help meet the overall needs (see Exhibit 4.1). Once funds are received from another source, the private fundraising goal can be reduced. The effect on the organization will be the same as if all the money was raised from donors, because needs will be met, but in this scenario other revenue sources were tapped to meet the gap caused by lowered gift expectations.

Sometimes campaign counting can be effected by adding revenue from another program. In universities, for instance, it is traditional to track funds from private sources separately from funds received from public sources.

EXHIBIT 4.1

Additional Sources of Revenue Used to Reach Campaign Goals

Public funds: City support, state support, or federal support.

Low-interest bonds.

Unrestricted bequests (received).

Expand revenue programs and reinvest revenue in the campaign needs.

Use Interest income on endowment to meet campaign needs.

Sell something (e.g., a piece of property or another asset held by the organization).

If your campaign counting policy only allows you to count gifts from private sources, that is, true philanthropy, consider breaking the bigger campaign goal out into two segments: one goal (reduced) identified with traditional philanthropy; another goal (the remainder) for the funds that are coming from the additional revenue source. In other words, it is not unethical or misleading to meet the campaign needs by other means if you tell everyone what you are doing.

 IN THE REAL WORLD

Beware of Counting Gifts that Are Not yet in Hand

A comprehensive campaign at a leading educational institution that shall not be named not only counted all cash and pledges received but added in the total face value (with no discount for age) of all bequest expectancies it was notified about (in other words, the campaign leaders counted bequests from living donors at full value).

There are accepted ways to count some portion of unrealized bequests in campaigns. For instance, some campaigns add a separate bequest total to their campaign report to build awareness of planned giving. Realized bequests (gifts from donors who have died) are usually counted, especially those made to campaign purposes. The Council for Advancement and Support of Education (CASE) has suggested rules for campaign counting that include discounting bequests, and stipulates that all bequests counted should be notarized with a copy of the will put on file with the university.

It is usually considered bad practice, however, to count all bequests at face value from living donors. Why? Three simple reasons:

❶ Bequest donors can change their minds, and there is no legal way to bind them to their earlier decision.

❷ The value of the gift will be reduced between the time that the gift is counted and the time that the institution receives it because current dollars are worth more than future dollars.

❸ The organization—far from having the resources to actually meet its current needs—is hobbled by having to wait 10, 20, 30, or more years to realize the gift.

Bad counting hurts the advancement operation's legitimacy within the organization, hurts the organization's ability to meet its current needs, and leaves donors with the impression that the organization does not need their money by exaggerating the amount of dollars raised. Do not be tempted to do it!

 TIPS AND TECHNIQUES

Methods for Changing Campaign Goals

- Keep the same goal but extend the timeline to reach it.

- Break a large goal up into smaller goals by taking campaign components apart and setting sequential goals for each segment of the campaign.

- Exclude or delay a component of the campaign that seeks funds with a long-term impact.

- Raise capital now and move endowment back to a second phase.

- Announce a campaign time-out for strategic planning.

- Reassess programs and needs and come back with a new goal based on new needs.

- Develop a set of reduced program budgets and needs, then cut the campaign to meet the new lower need levels.

- Add the annual fund to a larger campaign but reduce the overall goal by the amount added.

- Develop additional revenue programs and lower campaign goals to accommodate increased revenue from other sources.

Adjusting Gift Tables to Meet New Realities

Gift tables are visual representations of the traditional giving pyramid. They are charts that are used to illustrate the number of new gifts that are needed at each dollar level to meet the campaign goals. Most traditional campaigns plan for, and receive, fewer gifts at the top of the table and more gifts at the bottom, because this is naturally how their donor base is constructed. When a campaign begins to slow down, it often shows weakness at the top end of the gift table first, because the largest gifts become the hardest to raise when the times become tougher.

Learning a little about the construction of gift tables can be useful in adjusting the campaign for changing circumstances. It is possible to construct several very different gift tables for the same campaign. Consider Exhibits 4.2 and 4.3; both show gift tables for campaigns of $5 million. Campaign I requires a gift of $1 million at the top, while Campaign II projects three top gifts of $500,000.

EXHIBIT 4.2

Table of Gifts for a $5 Million Campaign with a Lead Gift of $1 Million (Campaign I)

Gift Level	# Prospects	# Gifts Needed	$ Raised	% of Total
$1,000,000	3	1	$ 1,000,000	20%
$ 500,000	6	2	$ 1,000,000	20%
$ 250,000	12	4	$ 1,000,000	20%
$ 100,000	18	6	$ 600,000	12%
$ 50,000	36	12	$ 600,000	12%
$ 25,000	60	20	$ 500,000	10%
$ 10,000	90	30	$ 300,000	6%
Totals	**225**	**75**	**$ 5,000,000**	**100%**

EXHIBIT 4.3

Table of Gifts for a $5 Million Campaign with 3 Lead Gifts of $500,000 (Campaign II)

Gift Level	# Prospects	# Gifts Needed	$ Raised	% of Total
$ 500,000	9	3	$ 1,500,000	30%
$ 250,000	12	4	$ 1,000,000	20%
$ 100,000	24	8	$ 800,000	16%
$ 50,000	48	16	$ 800,000	16%
$ 25,000	72	24	$ 600,000	12%
$ 10,000	90	30	$ 300,000	6%
Totals	**255**	**85**	**$ 5,000,000**	**100%**

Campaign I requires 225 prospects and 75 gifts, but Campaign II will require over 10 percent more prospects; it calls for 255 prospects for 85 gifts. The point to focus on is that Campaign II, the one with the smaller top gift, is actually a more difficult campaign to run, because it requires a larger number of lower level gifts to make up the gap of $500,000 missing at the top. (The difference between the top gift of $1 million in Campaign I and the $500,000 top gift in Campaign II is a gap of $500,000.)

Think about which of these examples fits your campaign better. In these gift tables we have used a standard campaign ratio of three prospects to one gift. Your ability to turn prospects into donors may run ahead or behind this ratio, so you will want to adjust the prospect numbers to reflect your experience. You must match your prospect pool to the number of donors needed at each level, starting from the top down. It quickly becomes obvious that there are significant trade-offs between Campaign I in Exhibit 4.2 and Campaign II in Exhibit 4.3.

Campaign I requires one top gift of $1 million. You may think that a gift at this level is not an option for your campaign right now, but before you dismiss it, make sure you have adequately cultivated and asked any prospects capable of a $1 million gift. In fact, one of the first considerations to make is that perhaps you can *go up* the gift table and find a gift of $2 million! Remember that one gift at the top takes the place of numerous gifts further down the scale.

This gift table strategy—moving gift levels up, not down—leads to one of the most important concepts in campaign work.

KEY CONCEPT

It is easier, more efficient, less expensive, and more productive to raise gifts at the upper end of the gift table than in the middle or at the bottom.

If your staff has been cut, your campaign budget axed, and the needs are still there, do not think smaller gifts, think bigger gifts. The leverage from one big gift will allow you to build momentum for your campaign, show success, drop the number of total prospects needed, and get that much closer to reaching the goal.

Recognition at What Price?

Most campaigns plan for recognition by setting specific prices on naming options in the programs or facilities that the campaign will fund. Recognition has become a popular way to motivate donors to make larger and larger gifts.

IN THE REAL WORLD

The University of Chicago placed a full-page advertisement in the *Wall Street Journal* to announce the naming of its business school for a donor in the fall of 2008. The school is now called the University of Chicago Booth

School of Business, or Chicago Booth, for short. It is named after donor and alumnus David Booth, who gave the university an unprecedented gift of $300,000,000 to endow the school.

According to an earlier announcement in the *Journal*, the money will be used to hire and retain professors and to expand publications in the school of business. Mr. Booth is the chief executive of the Dimensional Fund Advisors mutual fund and a 1971 graduate of the University of Chicago.

This is an exciting level of recognition that honors the donor of a huge gift. The naming of a school, college, campus, or other permanent entity provides the donor with highly visible recognition for the lifetime of the organization. Tying the donor's name forever to a prestigious school at one of our nation's top universities certainly conveys the importance and uniqueness of this gift. The full page ad in the *Wall Street Journal* is an indication of both the value of the gift and a nod to the donor, whose fortune was made in the financial world.

Setting prices for recognition can be tricky. This is another one of those areas where intimate knowledge of the prospect pool can help your campaign achieve success. When pricing naming opportunities, the campaign planner has to take into account a number of factors:

- The level of gifts expected and the number of gifts at each level.
- The attractiveness of various naming opportunities to donors.
- The potential for maximizing unique naming options, such as the exterior name on a building, which will be given to only one donor.
- The price that peer organizations have set for similar recognition.

In standard capital campaign practice, the exterior naming of a building carries the highest price. This price is often set based on a percentage of the total cost of the facility. The range of pricing for the external name can run from 25 percent to 50 percent or more of the total cost, with 33 percent being a common middle ground.

For example, if the building will cost $10 million, the exterior name could be priced anywhere from $2.5 million (25 percent) to $5 million (50 percent).

Your final decision will depend on several factors. The price might be moved up to $5 million if there is a donor who is capable of making a gift at that level. Based on our discussion in the last section, it is smarter to push at the top end of the gift table in order to save effort at the bottom. However, if no $5 million prospect is in the offing, it makes sense to drop to a lower price, perhaps $3 million, to secure a leadership gift.

It can be dangerous to fiddle with or negotiate prices once the campaign has begun, but it may become necessary to do so if no donor seizes the top naming opportunities. Moving the top recognition level up or down is usually done more easily than moving the price level on middle gifts, because in most cases the top gifts are unique to one or two donors. Thus donors cannot compare the amount they paid for similar recognition and discover that discounting has taken place.

It is also possible after the campaign is under way to add a new level of donor naming options at the low end of the scale. Let us say that your campaign has sold a number of naming opportunities at or above $25,000, and now the campaign is moving into its public phase. Adding recognition and naming options for gifts of $5,000, $10,000, and $15,000 to the mix might help to increase the average gift from donors at the low end of the scale, improving your chances of meeting the goal.

Thus, it is possible to change prices at the top, or to add new naming options at the bottom, of the campaign gift table even after the campaign has reached midstream. See Exhibits 4.4 and 4.5 to see how recognition prices can change to meet the gift levels actually encountered in a sample campaign. Capital Campaign A represents the initial campaign recognition plan, with one $5 million lead gift to name the exterior of the building. (Note that the original naming plan adds up to slightly more than $10 million in order to cover gift levels that might not be met.)

After 18 months of fundraising, the campaign planners find that they need to adjust the gift levels. No $5 million donor is in sight, and there are a number of lower level prospects who would respond well if they were to be recognized

EXHIBIT 4.4

Sample Recognition Table for Capital Campaign (A) with a $10 Million Goal

Naming Option	# Available	Price/Unit	Total
Exterior building name	1	$ 5,000,000	$ 5,000,000
Entrance atrium foyer	1	$ 2,000,000	$ 2,000,000
Main conference room	1	$ 750,000	$ 750,000
Secondary conference rooms	2	$ 250,000 each	$ 500,000
Large auditorium-style classrooms	2	$ 250,000 each	$ 500,000
Computer centers	2	$ 250,000 each	$ 500,000
Administrative offices	5	$ 100,000 each	$ 500,000
Regular classrooms	12	$ 50,000 each	$ 600,000
Total			**$10,350,000**

EXHIBIT 4.5

Sample Recognition Table for Capital Campaign (B) with a $10 Million Goal

Naming Option	Available	Price/Unit	Total
Exterior building name	1	$ 3,000,000	$ 3,000,000
Entrance atrium foyer	1	$ 2,000,000	$ 2,000,000
Main conference room	1	$ 750,000	$ 750,000
Secondary conference rooms	2	$ 250,000 each	$ 500,000

(Continued)

Large auditorium-style classrooms	2	$ 250,000 each	$ 500,000
Computer centers	2	$ 250,000 each	$ 500,000
Administrative offices	5	$ 100,000 each	$ 500,000
Regular classrooms	12	$ 50,000 each	$ 600,000
Small seminar rooms	10	$ 35,000 each	$ 350,000
Lobby areas	10	$ 25,000 each	$ 250,000
Break out rooms	15	$ 10,000 each	$ 150,000
Study carrels	70	$ 5,000 each	$ 350,000
Benches	20	$ 2,500 each	$ 50,000
Name on a permanent plaque	500	$ 1,000 each	$ 500,000
Total			**$10,000,000**

Changes between Exhibit 4.4 and Exhibit 4.5 are highlighted.

in some fashion. Capital Campaign B is the same campaign for a $10 million building, but now it has been adjusted to meet reality by lowering the top recognition level to $3 million, and adding $1.65 million in naming options at lower levels.

While making these changes will help to stimulate fresh donor activity, which is the goal of providing recognition in the first place, they also put more pressure on the lower end of the campaign. The new goals set for donors and dollars from $1,000 to $25,000 are very aggressive, but they have to be aggressive to make up for the $2 million that has been taken out of the top level naming opportunity.

Campaigns usually offer many other kinds of recognition beyond putting the donor's name on a room or building. There are schools that are named for substantial endowments, programs that are named for corporate sponsors, and individual donors whose names are engraved on plaques. All of the available options—lists, plaques, rooms, programs, signage, and web site banners—need to be spelled out in advance, explained to donors, and linked to specific gift levels.

TIPS AND TECHNIQUES

Ways to Recognize Endowed Gifts

Name a chair for a professor or teacher in honor of the donor or her family.

Consider more than one chair level. (For instance, name a Distinguished Chair for a higher level gift.)

Name the position of a director, dean, or executive level administrator.

Name the program being endowed, for example, the Jones Lecture Series.

Name a scholarship or fund that will be permanently endowed.

Name the school or unit being endowed.

Name buildings or rooms that are not reserved for capital campaign donors.

Name exterior spaces, like quads, fields, or an entire campus.

List donors to endowment on a permanent and prominent plaque.

List donors to endowment on the organization's web site.

Invite endowment donors to a special event for like-minded donors.

Create an endowment recognition society, like an annual fund society, for donors to endowment. Hold an annual event, list donors' names in print, and create a plaque to honor all donors above a certain level to endowment.

Summary

There are a variety of ways to change or modify the structure of a campaign once it is in progress. Key campaign components such as goals and timing can be announced initially as a range, with the final goal and timetable set after the campaign has completed the silent phase.

In the same manner, campaign gift tables and recognition opportunities can and should be altered when the campaign enters into difficulty. Take care to match changes in external fundraising goals with the costs of the needs that will be funded by the campaign, for example, if the campaign goal drops by $2 million, your organization will have $2 million less to spend on its needs.

Campaign plans should be changed with care so that an organization's constituents, along with the broader community, continue to respect the achievements and integrity of the nonprofit.

CHAPTER 5

The Human Element: Reengaging Board, Staff, and Volunteers

After reading this chapter, you will be able to:

- Convince your board to reinvest in the campaign.
- Motivate campaign volunteers.
- Measure staff productivity and improve morale.

Getting Your Board to Reinvest in the Campaign

When a campaign slows down or encounters difficulty, sometimes the first reaction of the executive director/CEO is to hide the facts from the board. It is natural to want to look good for the group that is responsible for the long-term health of the organization and, of course, it is the board that evaluates the work of the executive director. This instinct to cover up problems does not serve the organization well, however, because, as we will see, to some extent the resuscitation of the campaign lies in the hands of the board members themselves.

The board must be kept apprised of the facts about current fundraising progress, especially in times of trouble. First of all, to do otherwise is to act in a manner that is not straightforward and honest, a troubling approach in the best of times, which will backfire on management if fundraising revenues continue to decline. In addition, the board—which has a responsibility to not only give money but to get money—is often the best resource to help solve fundraising problems. And finally, the board can only share responsibility and engage in turning the campaign around if its members are fully informed.

KEY CONCEPT

The proper function of a nonprofit board member in the fundraising arena is to give *and* to get, that is, to ask others to give.

Boards have different policies for how much a board member should give and what other fundraising responsibilities membership might entail. There are boards where every member is told—upon recruitment—that the policy is for each member "to give or to get" $10,000. Other boards, notably at universities, expect much larger gifts from their board members and select only those who have the capacity to give $1 million or more. Many community nonprofits have boards that are composed of members who are not chosen for their wealth. These board members are usually encouraged to give a minimal amount, so that the organization can claim 100 percent participation from its board.

Whatever your organization suggests or requires in terms of giving, your board members should be intimately involved in fundraising, and especially so if you are in a campaign. We are not talking just about the development committee, or even the campaign committee. These groups do take charge of certain fundraising functions; they may set policy, review goals, approve needs, and assist with making calls.

In a successful nonprofit, the *entire* board should be kept abreast of overall fundraising and campaign progress. Issues that arise in these sectors should be brought specifically to the board's attention. Certainly, if the campaign has stalled, the entire board should be made aware of the problem.

Reassessing Board Membership

While the advancement function does not control board membership, the makeup of the board is critical to the success of the fundraising enterprise. You may want to take part in discussions with your board and executive leadership about the addition of new board members, the choice of board leaders, and the size of the board. In many organizations, nominating committees ask the advancement CEO for suggested names for new board members, for instance.

Even if your input is not sought or is not acted upon, help your board leadership by offering to prepare materials for board recruitment that spell out fundraising duties and responsibilities. Also ask your board and executive leadership if you can play a role in the orientation program for new board members. Your board members should understand the role that the board plays in campaign leadership from the beginning of their service to the organization.

You may want to reassess your board membership to keep it strong in order to help your organization ride out the recession. Think about making changes in board structure, membership, or recruitment procedures as you revamp your campaign. You might want to suggest a restructuring of the nominating process, setting up a new process for training future leaders, or expanding the board to include more national members.

TIPS AND TECHNIQUES

Reasons to Add New Board Members

- Broaden representation from different sectors of the community.
- Add diversity of ethnic background, age, sex, and/or religion.
- Increase geographic representation to support outreach efforts and fundraising.
- Provide representation from business sectors that are important to the campaign, for example, banking, real estate, energy, manufacturing, agriculture, or finance.
- Provide familiarity with nonprofit accounting and governance practices.
- Expand the next generation of leaders for the organization.

(Continued)

- Increase the number of members who are knowledgeable and passionate about the work of the organization.
- Add experienced fundraisers.
- Add more people of wealth who could be potential donors.

While it is important to have board members who bring a wide variety of skills, it is also important to have some members who can give large gifts and some who will ask for gifts—and these are not always the same people.

Many new board members complain that they are never told exactly what the expectations are for their involvement before they agree to join a nonprofit board. This area is rife for misunderstanding, especially when financial contributions are part of the equation. Think carefully about the expectations you have of your board and how you communicate these expectations to new board members. Some boards write out a set of board responsibilities and use these when recruiting new members (see Exhibit 5.1).

EXHIBIT 5.1

Example of Board Responsibilities to Use When Recruiting New Members

1. Every board member must "give or get" a minimum of $10,000 each year.

2. Board members are asked to participate in three areas of giving at the level of their capability: buying gala event tickets, participating in the annual fund, and making a campaign gift.

3. Board members are expected to participate in at least two out of four annual meetings and join at least two standing committees.

4. The term of service is five years, with the option of serving one additional term sequentially (if invited).

5. A minimum of a two-year hiatus is required after leaving the board before renomination is an option.

6. All members must adhere to the conflict of interest policy.

7. All new members must attend the board orientation session before the first meeting in the fall.

Reassessing Board Leadership

In tough times, board leadership is more important than ever. How can you measure the leadership quotient of your board? What steps can you take to promote better leadership? Are there new leaders who could be promoted? Take the time to review your board leadership and make a plan for strengthening it. Strong board leadership is a key to fundraising success, now more than ever.

TIPS AND TECHNIQUES

Measure the Leadership Quotient of your Board

Grade your board chair and leadership group (this may be the executive committee) on each of the following qualities using a scale of 1 to 5, with 1 high:

- Our leaders are active in our fundraising and campaign efforts.
- Our leaders have taken the time to fully understand the changing economy and its effect on our operations.
- Our leaders are helping us with plans to conserve scarce resources, that is, they are helping us to take quick and efficient action to adjust to lowered revenues.
- Our leaders are heading the effort to expand additional sources of revenue to replace those that might be lost.
- Our leaders are giving the time, energy, and financial support necessary to keep our organization strong.
- Our leaders are willing to strategize with us to look at new ways of approaching the campaign in order to reach success.

Key:

A low score, from 6 to 12, shows your board leadership quotient is strong.

A higher score, from 13 to 19, shows that some training on leadership development is needed. A score above 20 means that you should consider means for replacing the current leadership or look for a new job.

Steps to Promote Stronger Leadership

There are many tools, training programs, and workshops devoted to building board leadership skills. Look to the CASE web site at www.case.org/and the AFP web site at www.afpnet.org/for books and seminars offered in this field. In the current environment, it is critical to develop a high-functioning, well-trained board whose members communicate well with management and with each other.

If your board leadership quotient needs work, consider some of the following possibilities:

- Look for a fundraising seminar where board members and advancement officers are trained together. This will allow your group to work together on skills.

- Identify a consultant who can come in to work with your board members on leadership skills, planning, decision making, and fundraising skills.

- Identify a key volunteer or prior board chair who is well respected. Ask him to lead a session with the board leadership on changing board responsibilities and how to provide leadership in a challenging environment.

One popular option is to plan a board retreat for training and bonding. Plan a full day retreat that includes the board and key managers. Use the first half of the day to review board responsibilities, update long-range plans, and to evaluate your organization's progress toward the goals in your plan. In the afternoon, tie the planning session to funding needs, and develop new strategies together for restarting the campaign. Adjust fundraising goals if necessary with the leadership present.

You might also consider creating a "Crisis Leadership Team" including the immediate past chair, the current chair, and the upcoming chair of your board. To represent the management group, include the executive director/CEO, the head of finance, and the chief advancement officer. Meet with this group regularly to provide support for all major decisions affecting the organization during the crisis period.

Remember to keep communication channels open. Do not pull surprises on the board (such as changing the campaign goal or firing half the staff) without clear advance communication and input from the board leadership. Consider crisis communication techniques, such as weekly conference calls, daily e-mail updates, monthly lunch meetings, or other means of keeping communication flowing smoothly.

Start to identify new leaders with fresh ideas who are willing to work hard and who have a passion for your cause. Create ways to include these new leaders in a leadership group you can tap into, such as a "Young Leadership Council" or as a new advisory council. Add young leaders who seem most promising to your board now so that they can be more effective during this period of turmoil.

Seek Board Buy In for Any Changes in the Campaign

Ideally, your board will already be familiar with the campaign needs, goals, and progress to date through regular reports, either from the chief advancement officer or through the development committee. Your board should receive campaign results on a monthly basis at a minimum. You may want to consider more frequent reports if fundraising has slowed down. Some nonprofits are now updating their board leaders weekly on all fundraising trends, including campaign and annual fund results, so that the board is aware of current challenges.

The more the board as a whole is involved and informed about campaign issues, the better its response will be to pleas that it provide assistance and support.

Here are four specific ways that board members can assist the organization in the event of a stalled campaign:

1. *Review campaign analysis.* The board should be made aware of the internal analysis of campaign strengths and weaknesses. The board could receive a summary report of the analysis, perhaps in a retreat setting, where discussion is usually freer and more extensive than in a regular meeting. It is possible that one or more board members could be tapped to help conduct the analysis, if they present the right experience and skill set. The board as a whole is probably more likely to accept the analysis report if

one of its own members has been involved in preparing it (or has overseen its preparation).

2. **Set policy.** The board should play a lead role in the decision making process if deteriorating economic conditions require internal adjustments within the organization. This would include decisions on areas that affect the entire organization, such as staffing and budget cuts, construction delays, and changes in programs. Your board should also review changes in advancement strategies such as adjustments to campaign goals, needs, timing, recognition policies, pricing, and the case for support. The board is ultimately responsible for the fiduciary health of the organization, and these decisions will have a definite impact on your finances, both in the short term and over the long term.

3. **Open the door to new prospects.** Board members, who often play a leadership role in the community, are in a unique position to help revive your campaign by identifying new prospects. Work with them both individually and in small groups to review lists of past donors, foundation trustees, corporate officers, and donors to peer institutions. Their ability to gain access to decision makers across the community and open doors is more important to your organization now than ever before. Rally the troops, get them excited about your organization's needs, and put them to work!

4. **Make another gift.** Last but not least, board members are often the most likely source for new gifts. They already know and like the organization, and they have a personal interest in seeing the campaign succeed. Many of your board members probably have additional giving capacity, even if they have already made an initial gift or pledge to the campaign. Appeal to them on the basis of urgency and need, given the pressure of the weakened economy. Make sure that they understand that an all-out effort is being made to improve fundraising results before asking them to fill in the gap. Consider ways to approach the most capable donors for a second gift. For instance, weigh the possibility of a board giving challenge, a board match, or a similar motivational tool to help support a second ask.

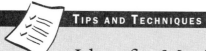

TIPS AND TECHNIQUES

Ideas for Motivating a Second Gift from Current Supporters

- Set up a challenge for current donors to reach a certain goal with second gifts.
- Solicit a match with the stipulation that all second gifts will be matched 1:1.
- Develop a new way to recognize second donors. For instance, offer them a special benefit, such as a limited print or a free table at an event.
- Sell up. Make a personal appointment with each donor to a new building to review the signage and selection of the room or space they have already agreed to name. Point out rooms or spaces that are priced at higher amounts and ask if they want to increase their gift to opt for the more expensive recognition.
- Ask all current donors to add one additional year to their pledges.
- Make a second appeal to donors based on a stronger and more urgent case.
- Show how needs have escalated for the organization's services due to the economic downturn.

If there are significant policy decisions that need to be addressed by the board concerning the future of the organization, especially decisions that involve campaign or fundraising results, hold a one-day retreat to review the relevant issues. Board retreats can help members to better understand the urgency of the needs and can encourage them to make an additional gift in support of the campaign.

Your board members should be given the time to fully explore the challenges of the current environment, delve into the analysis of the campaign results, and participate in decisions for the organization's future. These discussions will not only help the members to make the right policy decisions, they will also serve to cultivate the board for additional gifts. After the retreat, plan an individual meeting with each board member to ask for their support with an additional gift.

Using a Feasibility Study to Raise a $5 Million Gift

An independent school had been planning to build a new science center for two to three years. It updated its campus plan, bought some adjoining property, hired an architect, and worked with its faculty to develop an attractive set of plans for the perfect building they all wanted.

The school hired a fundraising consultant to conduct a feasibility study just as the markets were declining—bad timing, everyone said. The interviews caught the prospective donors at a time of great financial uncertainty. The study came back with the finding that the school could raise only $7 million toward the $12 million project.

The consultant presented a draft of the feasibility study results to a small group that included the head of school, several faculty, two board members, and the chairman of the board, who had been interviewed for the study and rated as a $1 million potential donor.

The reduced goal of $7 million from the feasibility study was met with disbelief. The head of school and her faculty were horrified that their dream was not going to be realized. The two board members present were not too surprised, because they had been seeing their own portfolios decline as the markets plunged. They began to urge a more pragmatic approach to redefining the school's needs in the sciences.

The chairman listened carefully, and then turned to the consultant. "How large a gift would be needed to close the gap so that we could build the building?" he asked. The consultant replied that her study showed that the project was short $5 million.

"Then I will do the $5 million myself," the chairman said to the astonished group. (And this is a good reason to have a feasibility study done for your campaign.)

Remember that board members and volunteers are going to be undergoing their own difficulties with the weak economy, and be patient with demands for time and money. It may help to identify those whose personal finances are in better shape and let others slide for a few months. Try to ascertain how your key volunteers and board members are faring in the recession. The more you know about their business and finances, the better able you will be to tap their time and resources in a personal and sensitive manner. Do not be afraid to ask your volunteers how they are faring—their answers might surprise you.

Now let us look at how volunteers beyond the board can be recruited, trained, and kept engaged in the work of the campaign.

Motivating Volunteers

Volunteers become even more important in the nonprofit world when budgets get tight. While many advancement professionals already have extensive experience in identifying, training, and rewarding volunteers, special attention needs to be paid at this time to recruit and retain the best of the best. Volunteers need good communication, meaningful assignments, and staff support to produce at the highest levels. Great campaign volunteers are especially prone to burnout, since they are often relied on heavily in making cultivation and solicitation calls.

Here are a few suggestions for recruiting and retaining new and/or experienced volunteers for your campaign effort:

- Conduct monthly information sessions for all volunteers to update them on campaign progress.

- Design and use a campaign volunteer handbook.

- Consider hiring an additional staff member (or promote an experienced volunteer) to be responsible for volunteer coordination and activity.

- Ask the board or campaign chair to host a volunteer appreciation event.

- Survey volunteers regarding their satisfaction with their experience and ask them for suggestions on how to involve others.

 TIPS AND TECHNIQUES

Campaign Volunteer Recognition Program

Volunteers should feel appreciated. Here are some ideas for recognizing their efforts:

- Send them a thank-you note after each call made on a prospect.
- List their names in the campaign newsletter (quarterly or annually).

(Continued)

- Thank them publicly at events.
- Host an annual volunteer luncheon to thank them for their efforts.
- Start a volunteer of the year award.
- Spotlight a volunteer on the campaign web site.
- Profile a volunteer in the campaign newsletter.
- Design a pin, T-shirt, or other type of apparel for volunteers only.

Strengthen Campaign Leadership

Sometimes campaign leadership needs to be reassessed. If your campaign chair is tired, ineffective, and beginning to avoid your phone calls, it is time to think about moving in a new direction. Campaign chairs can burn out, too, and who would blame them? It takes a great deal of responsibility and time to run a major campaign even in the best of times.

There are several options for replacing or augmenting a campaign chair who is showing signs of fatigue. Do not just ignore the issue and pretend it will go away. Here are some ideas for dealing with this issue effectively:

- Add one or two cochairs to support a campaign chair who has been serving alone.
- Create terms for your campaign chair; retire the first one after two years at the helm and bring in fresh leadership.
- Promote the campaign chair to become the honorary chair and replace her with two or three cochairs.
- Consider replacing a local campaign chair and committee with a new national campaign committee comprising volunteers from all over the country (or whatever regions your organization operates in).

Naming campaign cochairs instead of one single chair has become a popular idea, especially in large comprehensive campaigns. The concept is that one person only has so much reach and influence in the community, whereas two or three individuals serving as cochairs will double or triple the number of prospects that can be reached. In addition, by selecting cochairs from different industry or social circles, new prospects can be brought into the campaign by diversifying the leadership.

National representation (or regional representation, depending on your organization's makeup) on the campaign leadership team can also be a very effective method of bringing new energy and new prospects into the fold. Consider identifying city chairmen, state chairmen, or regional chairs to broaden your fundraising efforts.

Bringing in new blood is a good way to rebuild enthusiasm in a campaign where the leaders are flagging. If your campaign leadership needs some propping up, use one of these methods to get things back on track.

Avoid Volunteer Burnout

Burnout can be deadly for a campaign volunteer, and the ones who burn out are the ones called on over and over again because they are so good. You can counteract this tendency with some advance planning.

It is important to grow new volunteers. Ask your top volunteers to train new recruits on the road by taking them on prospect calls. Pair the best volunteers with trainees to grow an experienced volunteer cadre. And keep the busy work to a minimum for your best solicitors—they are hard to replace. Rotate routine assignments such as signing letters, reviewing lists, and attending events so different volunteers get used to being called upon.

Reenergizing the foot soldiers can also be a matter of communication and training. Keep volunteers posted on changes in the campaign and ask their opinions on issues that arise. Campaign volunteers can make a great informal focus group for testing changes in the case or for reviewing printed materials.

Keep your volunteers current. Provide workshops or group sessions on new strategies, such as integrating the annual fund into campaign solicitations. Find appropriate training topics, such as how to present planned giving options or the best ways to close a gift. The better prepared your volunteers are to face tough questions from tough prospects, the faster your campaign will turn around.

Where to Look for New Volunteers

There will come a time when, through attrition or the need to reenergize the group, your organization will need to find new campaign volunteers. Where to start? Review the sources in Exhibit 5.2 to see if any of these concepts would work for your organization. Remember that the better your volunteers feel about their work with your group, the more likely you are to attract new, energized volunteers to join the effort.

Volunteers can be found through a variety of means, including placing an ad in the organization's newsletter or on its web site. Do not forget that word of mouth is also productive, since many volunteers like to work with people they already know. Ask your current volunteers to bring a new prospect to a holiday party or luncheon. And as you make your way through the calendar of events you attend in your community, keep an eye out for

---

EXHIBIT 5.2

How to Find New Campaign Volunteers

- Promote successful annual fund volunteers to the campaign.

- Get lists of current and past volunteers from other program managers in your organization and send them letters asking for their help.

- Ask current volunteers for names of friends or family who might enjoy volunteering.

- Ask recent donors if they want to volunteer.

- Write an article in your newsletter outlining the need, the skills, and the activities that volunteers will be asked to take on.

- Hold a thank-you event for volunteers and ask them to each bring a good prospect.

- Put up a notice on your web site for prospective volunteers to call you.

- When you attend community events and holiday parties, be on the lookout for good prospective volunteers.

capable volunteers whom you might be able to steal. After all, all is fair in love, war, and fundraising!

In the Real World

The Volunteer Who Gave All She Had to Give

An art museum had an elderly docent who was a regular volunteer. She loved showing people around the collection in her little rubber-soled shoes. A modest person, she lived and dressed simply, and appeared to be a woman without much wealth. Her annual gift to the museum was at the minimum level of $60 for a membership.

When the docent passed away, the staff and volunteers mourned her loss. But to their surprise, her lawyer called to report a tremendous bequest: She had left the museum her entire estate, which totaled over $1.3 million!

The museum rejoiced and put up a plaque in the volunteer room in her honor. They also dedicated a newsletter to her story. Even though no one had realized her giving potential when she was active with the museum, she had been treated well and thanked often. The museum reaped what it had sown from maintaining good relationships.

Improve Staff Morale and Productivity

The ability to motivate and support advancement staff is not the only responsibility of the advancement CEO, but success with this task will make the CEO's life easier and bring in more money for the nonprofit. There are several factors that go into making the advancement staff more productive.

Make the Case to Keep Productive Staff Members

First, in an environment where scaling back on staff may be a knee-jerk response to financial difficulty, make sure that the team you are motivating is the team you will stick with. The advancement CEO should be actively engaged in showing management (and the board) why it is important to hold the advancement team together during a financial downturn. Consider an argument based on these points:

- *It takes money to raise money:* Calculate the cost per dollar raised for your campaign. Make sure to include publications, travel, events, and so forth in addition to staff salaries. Prove that the advancement staff is paying for itself many times over. (If you cannot prove that, you should cut your budget.)

- *Strong relationships with donors take time to develop and mature:* Cutting staff who work directly with donors should be a last resort. The relationships they have developed with donors are worth a great deal to your organization and will be worth more to a competitor.

- *Ask for more time:* In the current environment it is taking longer to close large gifts. Donors cannot predict how their assets will perform. Economic uncertainty is the enemy of the campaign. Set a timeframe in which to measure progress, refocus on goals that can be achieved, and keep the staff to make it happen.

- *If you have to cut, keep the best performers:* Take charge of decisions to cut staff; do not sit passively and let it happen to you. Keep the best performers and look for flexibility in skills—fewer staff members may have to cover more advancement areas.

Measure Staff Productivity

It is important to have the capability to measure staff productivity in order to motivate staff and, if necessary, to make decisions on who to keep and who to let go.

Measurement of campaign prospect activity has come a long way from the old boxes with index cards for each prospect that used to be the staple of campaign tracking. Now, with development information systems that can track calls, moves, asks, and gifts, performance and activity levels can be directly measured. Make use of the tracking systems that have been put in place and make sure that staff members keep their activity up to date.

KEY CONCEPT

Establish a rule that says if an action taken with a prospect has not been entered into the prospect tracking system, it did not take place.

If the organization you work with has not put a measurement system in place yet, review this section to learn how to measure and quantify staff productivity.

Structurally, the major gifts staff usually is responsible for making the field calls on campaign prospects. These staff members may report to a director of major gifts, a campaign manager, or directly to the chief advancement officer. In some multidivisional organizations, such as a university, hospital, or other nonprofit with numerous independently budgeted units, each division has a major gift officer reporting separately to the director/dean of each unit. Responsibility for productivity measurement rests at the supervisory level, one step up from the campaign field staff.

Supervising campaign staff members is like running the sales staff of a large company. Staff members need to be carefully motivated, trained, compensated, and directed, but all with a light touch. If the supervisory role is too heavy handed, then the entrepreneurial spirit will be beaten of the group, leaving the organization with a team that spends more time making excuses than making appointments. On the other hand, too little supervision can lead to cutting corners, conflicts of interest, and prospect calls that do not bring in gifts.

Be sure to implement an even-handed approach in measuring staff activity that takes into account the assignment of prospects. A staff member with 250 prospects spread all over the country will have a different contact rate than a staff member who is working with 100 prospects in his hometown.

The timing of movement of prospects through cultivation to the closing of the gift is also a measurable item. If the average time it takes in your campaign to move one prospect from identification to closing the gift is 12 to 14 months, then most of the staff should be able to meet this range for most of their prospects. There are exceptions to every rule, but cultivating forever is not a choice in the successful campaign. Watch out also for the reverse situation; it is possible by studying timing and gift records to determine if one staff member is rushing prospects to the ask, bringing in gifts that are smaller than expected.

TIPS AND TECHNIQUES

AFP Code Regarding Compensation for Development Officers

AFP has long regarded the payment of a percentage of the gift amount to development officers as an unethical practice. This is the actual language from the compensation section of the AFP Code of Ethical Principles and Standards of Professional Practice (amended 2004):

> Members shall not accept compensation that is based on a percentage of contributions; nor shall they accept finder's fees.

> Members may accept performance-based compensation, such as bonuses, provided such bonuses are in accord with prevailing practices within the members' own organizations, and are not based on a percentage of contributions.

> Members shall not pay finder's fees, or commissions or percentage compensation based on contributions, and shall take care to discourage their organizations from making such payments.

TIPS AND TECHNIQUES

How to Measure Campaign Staff Productivity

- Assign prospects by name to each staff member.
- Assign regions or areas of responsibility to each staff member.
- Set clear standards for what constitutes a contact with a prospect.

- Set quarterly goals for contacts with prospects.
- Install a moves management system to track all contacts with prospects.
- Set annual goals for dollars raised.
- Meet monthly or quarterly with each staff member to review progress.
- Give credit where credit is due. Most campaign gifts are a team effort.

Of course there are other staff members who contribute to campaign success, and productivity measurements also can be developed for these areas.

Proposal writers can be measured on the number of proposals completed, with a factor for the length and complexity of proposals. Track the percentage of proposals that get funded. While there are other factors that determine funding decisions, over time, the top proposal writers will have a higher percentage of their work funded.

Prospect researchers can be measured on the quantity and quality of research reports. While an ongoing count can be kept of new prospects identified and how many actually make a gift, it is difficult to attribute the gift activity directly back to the researcher's efforts. Still, the researcher who steadily unearths new names of prospects who go on to become donors is a valuable commodity and should be recognized for her high productivity.

 TIPS AND TECHNIQUES

How Not to Motivate Campaign Staff

Most nonprofits do *not* pay campaign staff a percentage of the gifts they bring in. There are several reasons for this:

- Paying a percentage of the gift to the solicitor is unethical according to AFP guidelines (see AFP Compensation Code nearby).
- Other team members who contribute to a successful solicitation—such as researchers and writers—do not get extra compensation.
- Volunteers and executive level staff, such as the executive director/CEO, do not get extra compensation for their fundraising work.

(Continued)

- Donors do not want a portion of their gift going to any purpose other than the one for which the donation was directed.
- Many gifts are the result of long-term relationships developed over years with the donor and cannot be attributed to the work of one staff member.
- Staff members would be motivated to close small gifts quickly in order to maximize compensation and could miss out on larger, lifetime gifts that take longer to cultivate and close.

Reward Staff Members for a Job Well Done

If your organization wants to reward top achievers on the campaign staff for a job well done, consider the following ideas:

- Set up an annual bonus system for reaching established goals, using goals that are financial and activity based.
- Hire at the going market rate and give appropriate annual raises.
- Provide perks that relate to the job, ranging from a company car to country club memberships.
- Provide staff members who travel often with company laptops, cell phones with e-mail capability, and other accoutrements of modern life on the road.
- Give credit to campaign staff members who are productive by praising them at board meetings, campaign meetings, and events.
- Promote from within so that staff members see a path for future advancement.
- Consider rewarding top performers with nonfinancial rewards, such as reserved parking, a personal day off, or access to a special benefit, and ask the executive director/CEO to write them a personal letter of thanks.

KEY CONCEPT

Your organization has invested heavily in building relationships between your donors and your staff, so you have to keep the staff in order to keep those relationships viable.

How Many Staff Members Do You Need to Run a Campaign, Anyway?

It can be difficult to assess how large a staff is needed to run a campaign. Most campaign managers look first at the number of prospects they need to cultivate and solicit to make the campaign numbers work. This means going back to the table of gifts and estimating how many prospects are needed for the remainder of the campaign.

New prospect tracking systems (one component of the development information system) make it easier than ever before for one staff member to manage or work with a large number of prospects. The number of prospects assigned to each staff member should probably fall somewhere in the range of 100 to 250 prospects per person, depending on factors like where the prospects live, how engaged they are with the organization, whether they have ever given before, and how much cultivation has already taken place.

Experience with the post-Katrina crisis in New Orleans proved beyond a doubt that nonprofits can run successful campaigns with a smaller number of full-time advancement staff members than had previously been thought. A combination of commitment to the cause, desperation, urgency, and the willingness to work long hours are major factors in filling in for missing staff. Beware, though, because after three years of working 10- and 12-hour days, there are many cases of staff burnout.

 IN THE REAL WORLD

A nonprofit in post-Katrina New Orleans needed to raise $18 million for a capital campaign to rebuild its facility, which had been completely destroyed in the flooding that followed the levee break. It had very little money available for overhead. This is how the organization structured the staffing for its campaign:

❶ **Full-time director of development:** Made calls, wrote proposals, directed volunteers, oversaw preparation of campaign materials.

(Continued)

② Full-time development assistant: Entered gifts in the data base, wrote thank-you letters, produced reports, scheduled meetings.

③ Campaign consultant: Worked an estimated 20 hours/month on a contract basis; assisted with strategy, prospects, materials, and volunteer direction.

④ Contract prospect researcher: Hired to research top prospect names and top previous donor names on a contract basis; only used in first three months.

⑤ Contract graphic designer: Prepared all materials, including campaign folder, logo, video, and stationery.

⑥ Contract events coordinator: Hired one person to manage events and coordinate volunteers on a contract basis.

⑦ Electronic prospect screening provider: Ran the nonprofit's database once through an electronic prospect screening program.

⑧ Direct mail experts: Hired an external consultant to handle all preparation and mailing of direct mail for annual operations.

⑨ Volunteer cochairs and campaign committee: Volunteers made all cultivation and solicitation calls on prospects, sometimes with CEO or development director, sometimes in teams, sometimes alone.

The campaign was run with two full-time staff in advancement and seven contract employees, who came in and out of the program as needed. Volunteers handled the remainder of the tasks. The campaign raised over $12 million in its first 18 months at an average cost of less than 3 cents on the dollar.

 IN THE REAL WORLD

The chief advancement officer at a small college planned a vacation with her family on a cruise ship. Just before she left for the trip, she discovered that a colleague at a peer institution had a spouse who worked with the cruise company. The colleague arranged through her spouse for a special VIP status that gave the family wonderful perks, such as free champagne and free passes to shows.

The fundraising executive came home from the vacation rested and grateful that her friend had done so much to add pleasure to their cruise. Grateful, that is, until she discovered that while she was gone, her "friend" had hired away her most productive major gift staff member!

Summary

Tough times call for strong campaign and board leadership. Make sure that your board and campaign leaders are well informed, decisive, and ready to take on the challenges of the current environment. Consider ways to augment or diversify your board leadership to help your organization deal with pressing fundraising issues.

Volunteers can form the backbone of a nonprofit when they are properly selected, trained, and motivated. Make plans to use volunteers more but also to develop better methods of training and supervision so that they can do their best work for you. Look at bringing in new volunteers to bring new energy to your campaign efforts and to help face new challenges.

Finally, make sure that your staff in the advancement area is being motivated appropriately. Make use of productivity measurements to evaluate and reward your most effective staff members. Your advancement staff members have developed strong relationships with key prospects for your organization, and finding ways to make them more productive may serve your organization better than firing them. If you must downsize the advancement staff, look at ways to outsource specific skill areas so that your campaign and fundraising needs can still be met.

CHAPTER 6

Desperately Seeking Donors: Prospect Identification, Cultivation, and Solicitation

After reading this chapter you will be able to:

- Identify additional prospects through prospect research.
- Improve your cultivation strategies for prospects.
- Develop additional skills for the solicitation and closing of gifts.

Improve Your List through Prospect Research

If a campaign is lagging, its troubles often can be traced back to the prospect sector. Whether the issue is not enough prospects, gifts that are too small, or a lack of leadership prospects, the answer lies in developing a broader and deeper prospect pool. But how does an organization go about doing that? The answer is in prospect research.

Prospect research is the term used for the methodology of finding, collating, and interpreting publicly available information to identify campaign prospects, that is those who are most likely to be your potential donors.

A strong researcher is the backbone of a successful campaign. If you have good researchers, keep them! If you do not, consider promoting a current administrative staff member to the research position from within. With time and access to professional training seminars, a prospect researcher can be trained on the job, and finding someone who is already familiar with your prospects is a plus.

A professional prospect researcher should offer a specific set of skills. Look for the ability to do detail work, good organization skills, and strong computer capabilities. Determination, focus, curiosity, and the patience to find information and put it all together are important qualities for success in the research field. Finding a person of the highest level of integrity is also a key requirement. The researcher will need to work closely with volunteers, board members, and staff to collect, process, and organize confidential information about prospects.

Expand Your Prospect List

Your first job is to expand your current pool of potential supporters. Prospects are people or organizations (including foundations and corporations) that, first and foremost, have the means to make a substantial gift to your campaign. No matter how much a prospect loves the work of your organization, he cannot make a meaningful financial contribution without the financial wherewithal to do so. So the first rule of prospecting is to look for wealth.

How much wealth is needed to make a gift? National studies of donor behavior show that most Americans give between 2 percent and 5 percent of their annual income to charity each year. For example, a professional woman who makes $80,000 a year is likely to make total donations of gifts ranging from $1,600 (2 percent × $80,000) to $4,000 (5 percent × $80,000) per year. Her capability will be higher if she is married to a spouse who is also earning a good income or if she has other sources of funds.

Therefore, with this prospect (without knowing about additional sources of funds) you might ask for a gift of $2,500 in one year (toward the middle of her giving capability range). This amount is based on the assumption that she will also be making gifts to other nonprofits, so your organization will not receive the total amount of her gift capability. It might be possible, when asking her for a special gift to a campaign, to ask this prospect for $25,000, or $5,000 × 5 years, and still meet with success. However, a pledge at this level would be a stretch for this prospect. She would probably need to have access to other sources of income to make a pledge at this level.

Let us look at what it takes to make a gift of $100,000 to your campaign. If the $100,000 is pledged over 5 years, you would be asking for $20,000 per year. The prospect's income level would have to be somewhere between $400,000 and $1 million *per year* to meet this gift level, if they were planning to give out of income (2 percent of $1 million is $20,000, and 5 percent of $400,000 is $20,000, so the income range would have to be between $400,000 and $1 million to make a gift of this size).

There are not many people who have an annual income at this level! If the prospect's income is below $400,000 per year, research would need to produce evidence of other sources of funds to justify an ask of $100,000. These other sources could include a spouse's income, family assets, a personal foundation, an inheritance, substantial noncash assets that produce income (such as real estate holdings) or a business whose assets could be accessed to make the gift.

Giving from assets, as opposed to giving from income, has recently become much less attractive to donors because of the tremendous decline in market value of many stocks. Stock gifts to charitable organizations are usually made from securities that have gained in value, allowing the donor to avoid paying capital gains tax on profits from the sale. If there are no profits to be realized from the sale of a stock (because its value has declined), there will be no capital gains tax, thus removing the incentive to give away the stock. Be sure to read the section in Chapter 2 on planned giving, which provides some tools to work with donors who are giving from assets.

 KEY CONCEPT

The first rule in prospecting is to look for wealth. The second rule is to look for a tie or connection to your organization.

EXHIBIT 6.1

Look for These Possible Ties When Identifying Individuals for Your Prospect List

- The prospect already gives to an organization that does the same work your nonprofit does.

- The prospect is a friend, relative, business associate, or colleague of someone who is already a donor to your campaign.

- The prospect lives in the community where the work of your organization is carried out.

- The prospect has given to your organization before.

- The prospect has shown some interest in your organization, such as attending an event, volunteering, visiting the site, buying a membership, or visiting the web site.

- The prospect has a family member or close friend who has benefited from a service your organization provides.

Exhibit 6.1 gives some guidelines for identifying prospects for your organization. Look for candidates who already have indicated some philanthropic interest in the cause or mission that your organization serves. Also be aware of any personal ties or relationships that exist between the prospect and someone who is already involved and giving to your organization.

Finding "Suspects" for Your Campaign

There are many additional sources for prospect names, but many of those names may have no apparent tie to your organization. In order to save yourself and your volunteers from wasting time cultivating prospects who have absolutely no interest in your organization, these cold prospect names should be considered "suspects" and vetted in some way before your organization uses valuable time and energy on them.

Reviewing lists of potential suspects with board members and campaign volunteers is often the best way to identify real prospects. This process of list review makes use of your volunteers' knowledge of the community and their personal connections. Prepare lists of potential suspects that are clear, easy to read, and identify as much as is known about the names for your list reviewers. For instance, note any small gifts that have been made to your organization already from these sources, because that might indicate a potential area of interest.

TIPS AND TECHNIQUES

Sources for "Cold" Prospect Names, or "Suspects"

- Identify corporations that conduct significant business in your community.
- Research national foundations that give to your interest area, for example, education or the arts.
- Develop a list of the names of wealthy individuals in your community from newspaper reports or from donor lists to other organizations.
- Look up all the family foundations in your community.
- Buy selected lists from a reputable list broker.
- Swap donor lists with similar organizations.
- Review names from the annual reports published by peer organizations.
- Review the list of vendors to your organization.
- Read the business news in your region and identify those who have started, bought, or sold companies.

IN THE REAL WORLD

The *Wall Street Journal* identified a list of "recession resistant industries" in an article dated December, 22, 2008, called "Avoiding the Ax: Where the Jobs Are." Your research efforts might focus on prospects in these fields:

Hospitals

Insurance

(Continued)

Accounting

Bankruptcy law

Consulting on crisis management

Health care

Education

Engineering: environmental, biomedical, civil, aerospace, and industrial

The *Journal* also identified the hardest hit areas in the same article. These are the sectors to watch out for:

Financial services

Real estate

Manufacturing

The process of prospect screening and wealth identification has been made much more scientific in recent years by the growth of companies that provide electronic prospect screening services. Do not assume that you can just enter any name in Google and come out with specialized information. Most of these services provide access to electronic databases that are not available unless you pay to join.

Electronic Prospect Screening

Electronic prospect screening has become a popular method for prioritizing a prospect list. As more information becomes available online, firms have begun to offer electronic methods of screening large numbers of prospect names in one computer run. These services are available for a fee, often based on the number of names screened. The prospect screening firms rely on publicly available data, like U.S. Securities and Exchange Commission insider stock holdings and contribution lists to political parties or candidates, so most of them will come up with similar information on a prospect name. They also have access to proprietary lists and internally held databases that can help to distinguish one firm from another.

As you research firms, ask the representative to run a free test using names in your own database. The results will help you see what information you could glean if you were to pay for the service. Data output formats and ease of use should also be part of the decision process as you determine which vendor to use. If you want the data you will receive to be loaded into your development information system, test this capability ahead of time. Reams of computer reports sitting on a shelf are not the most useful way to make this information available to campaign staff members.

Usually an electronic prospect screening service will be able to provide more information, on a much faster basis, than a staff researcher could provide working on his own.

Most electronic prospect research firms get their information from publicly available sources. While many of their sources are available to your research staff, some have a fee attached, and your staff will be slower in accessing this type of information for a large number of prospects than the big firms are. The screening firm can take your entire database and run it against several databases concurrently, rating prospects based on a series of factors. Some firms give you control over the factors or the weighting system used so that you can have them sort prospects to your own specifications.

Electronic screening should be viewed as one step in the prospect research process rather than as a substitute for the prospect researcher. Screening is a quick way to highlight key prospect or suspect names and to prioritize a list. It is not a substitute for intensive personal research on prospects. Electronic prospect screening will not tell you what a prospect is passionate about, it will not tell you if he is in the middle of a nasty divorce, and it will not tell you that he just lost his shirt in a new business.

Prospect researchers need good online tools (see Exhibit 6.2 for a list of common sources for prospect research). In combination with an electronic screening program, the researcher using these tools should be well positioned to determine which prospects get moved up to the next tier to receive personal attention from staff or volunteers.

EXHIBIT 6.2

Prospect Researchers Often Use These Sources

- Standard and Poor's (information on publicly held companies)

- Dun & Bradstreet (includes data on private companies)

- Real estate holdings (often provided by LexisNexis)

- LexisNexis Development Universe (online search capability that provides access to newspaper articles and other public information, searchable by name)

- Foundation guides (e.g., GuideStar or the Foundation Directory)

- SEC data on insider stock trading (used for researching corporate officers and large stock holders in public companies)

- Marquis Who's Who listings (provides personal biographical data)

Screening and Rating Sessions

Another common method of narrowing down prospect lists is to utilize prospect screening and rating sessions. Screening and rating sessions entail the organized review of lists of prospects by small groups of volunteers. Live screening sessions can be used in addition to electronic screening, or they can take the place of electronic screening.

Screening and rating session participants are asked to use their personal knowledge of the individuals being screened to identify prospects who might be able to make a gift to the campaign at a specified level. Participants should be asked to rate the prospect for a gift (you supply the appropriate rating levels), share any information that might be known about their wealth or giving patterns, and whether they are willing to "open the door" to the prospect to someone from the nonprofit. Volunteers who screen and rate prospects should be reassured that they do not have to ask the prospects whom they identify for money unless they wish to do so.

Screening in groups is sometimes done silently, with each member of the group working on her own list, or it can be conducted out loud, with all members of the group contributing to a discussion about each name on the list. Invite only those who already give to (or who are close to the work of) your organization. This is a great way to use boards and advisory councils to help expand the prospect pool for the campaign.

Sometimes volunteers are reluctant to share personal or financial information about prospects in front of others. Make sure that your letter inviting the participants to the session states clearly what the purpose of the meeting will be. If privacy is still an issue, arrange a private meeting with your volunteer to gather the information in a confidential setting.

TIPS AND TECHNIQUES

Conducting a Prospect Screening and Rating Session

1. Identify a small group to invite to the session as well as a session host. Consider holding sessions in different locations, 10 key cities, for instance.

2. Have the host invite the group to the session with a letter that explains the purpose clearly.

3. Hold sessions in a private setting, such as a corporate boardroom, a home, or a hotel meeting room (ask your host to find a place).

4. Arrange prospect lists into appropriate sectors, such as business field, geographic area, or age (for example, class year for universities and schools).

5. Provide a staff member to introduce the session, explain the campaign and its needs, and show a campaign video if one is available.

6. Assure the participants of confidentiality.

7. Screening can be conducted silently, with each member of the group working on his own list, or out loud, with everyone reviewing the same list.

(Continued)

8 Prepare the lists with boxes to check beside each name. Ask questions like these:

- How much could the prospect give? (Identify different levels to check off.)

- Does the participant know anything about the prospect that they can share with you? (A checked box will trigger a follow-up call after the session.)

- Is the participant willing to introduce the prospect to a representative from the organization, that is, open the door?

9 Thank them and ask the participants to support the campaign.

10 Set up a system to organize, process, and enter the information into the development information system for use by staff and researchers.

Prospecting for Foundations

Prospecting for foundations is a different ballgame from finding wealthy and connected individuals. Foundations are required to give away about 5 percent of their assets yearly to receive tax benefits. When the assets go down, the foundation's giving remains at the 5 percent level, but the 5 percent is calculated on a smaller base. Therefore there will be a substantial drop in foundation giving over the next few years due to the loss of value of investments in the stock market. However, foundations will still have to give away money, even if the amount is reduced, so they are inherently good prospects.

A good resource is the Foundation Directory Online, which is an online fee-for-service provider of information on over 95,000 foundations and corporate donors (see http://fconline.fdncenter.org/ for prices and services). In addition to profiles of each foundation, Foundation Directory Online provides electronic links to individual foundations' web sites and to their annual IRS 990s, which list useful information like names of trustees, which nonprofits received gifts, and amounts given in the relevant year.

Foundation Directory Online also provides a variety of useful search capabilities, including the capacity to search the entire database for the name of a trustee, a specific word or phrase, or by grants awarded. This last option allows users to find grants that have been given to organizations that do similar work to their own nonprofit. Also be sure to use the geographic feature, which allows users to review all foundations based in their own community or region.

The foundation world is generally divided into two distinct kinds of foundations. Local family foundations are groups that usually have trustees who are members or friends of the donating family. Many family foundations give broadly in their own communities, and most of them prefer knowing to whom they are giving. With this type of foundation, you will gain your best advantage by finding someone connected to your campaign who knows the family, or by making an effort to cultivate a family member directly and involving her in the work of your organization.

National foundations that make grants in areas of interest across the country (or across the globe) operate on a more formal, professional basis. National foundations, at least the big ones like Ford, Mellon, Gates, and Rockefeller, usually hire professional program officers and have a larger, prominent board that oversees operations and sets the agenda for the foundation's giving. Most of these foundations have their own web sites with extensive information about past grant activities, interest areas, how to apply, and who to contact for questions.

When working with national foundations, I recommend finding a professional grant writer who has experience with these kinds of grants. The requirements for proposals can be onerous, and sometimes smaller nonprofits struggle to meet the foundations' expectations for documentation of needs, finances, plans, programs, populations, and so forth.

Most national foundations have identified areas of support to which they prefer to give. Some may fund health care, while others will fund arts and cultural programs. Some will identify geographic preferences for their giving. They also will indicate what types of giving they will support, including endowment, capital, unrestricted, and/or programmatic funding.

Be sure before beginning to work on a grant of this type that your nonprofit meets all the requirements for the program you are applying for. It is wise to make a phone call or a personal visit with a foundation program director to discuss your project before taking the time to prepare the entire proposal—it can save you a lot of headaches.

Corporate Prospecting

Many companies are ready to support nonprofits, either as part of their mission, or to connect their name to a cause or mission that will resonate with their customers. It can be difficult, however, to determine where to start in identifying corporate prospects.

Consider buying a list from your local business newspaper. For instance the New Orleans weekly paper, *New Orleans City Business*, provides (for a fee) electronic versions of lists compiled by the staff each year. These lists are provided in useful categories, such as the top 100 private companies, or the top 50 banks in the region, listed by assets. Corporate officers are also listed.

Ask your campaign volunteers, board members, and advisory committee members to review these local business lists. A local business is more likely to give in its own community and to give to someone it knows. Corporate prospects can be assigned to volunteers, cultivated, and solicited just like individual prospects; however, the assets with which they make their gifts are more likely to come directly out of the business. (See Exhibit 6.3).

With corporate giving, there is often a connection between using business assets for charitable purposes and gaining visibility for the corporation. Companies are more likely to want to have visible recognition opportunities or to sponsor a program or activity with your organization. Some nonprofits seek corporate sponsorships for events rather than directing their giving toward a capital campaign for this reason.

National and international corporate prospects can be harder to pinpoint. Some large multinational companies have created corporate foundations, such as The Coca-Cola Foundation, Inc., which has its own professional staff, a separate board from that of the company, and defined giving interests. These can be searched for and accessed just like national foundations.

The Top 10 U.S. Foundations by Assets

1. Bill and Melinda Gates Foundation

2. Howard Hughes Medical Institute

3. The Ford Foundation

4. The Robert Wood Johnson Foundation

5. J. Paul Getty Trust

6. The William and Flora Hewlett Foundation

7. W.K. Kellogg Foundation

8. Lilly Endowment Inc.

9. John D. and Catherine T. MacArthur Foundation

10. The David and Lucile Packard Foundation

Copyright © Foundation Center 2008.

Other companies give out of corporate profits, with the dollar amount available changing each year. Sometimes the best contact is with the corporate marketing department, which identifies suitable PR and recognition options for the company. It is best to study the corporate web site to gain a better understanding of the giving options that a specific company may offer.

Once again, even with an international corporation, your best bet is to have a personal connection or to make a personal connection with someone high up. Corporate officers who have family ties to your institution can be powerful advocates, and so can CEOs who have experience with someone who has been a user of your services. This is another area where prospect research can be extremely useful; if your researcher can identify ties to corporate officers, you are ahead of the game.

Corporate donors (and even some foundation donors) have moved steadily toward requiring a written gift contract in return for a contribution. With public companies, there is the need to show stockholders that charitable gifts are being made to benefit the company in some manner. The contract might spell out a marketing campaign, or create a specific tie to the naming rights of the program being publicized. Often, contractual obligations cover elements such as the number and type of PR vehicles to be used, size of type, the exact name to be used, the duration of the agreement, and other elements that affect the corporation's ability to gain market advantage with the gift.

Some companies seek a competitive advantage by aligning themselves with the mission of a nonprofit when they are actually neglectful or even abusive in the field of work represented by the charity. For instance, an environmentally challenged mining company might want to link its charitable giving programs to green organizations in an effort to launder its name and activities.

 TIPS AND TECHNIQUES

Beware of Inappropriate Corporate Partnerships!

The most valuable thing an organization has is its reputation. It is difficult to regain the public's trust once it has been compromised. If you have the slightest hesitation about the propriety of approaching a certain business sector or a specific company, be sure to check with the executive committee of your board. It is easier to put a hold on such a gift at the front end than to risk embarrassment (and worse) once the gift has been signed and delivered.

Improve Prospect Cultivation Strategies

Finding new names and identifying potential ties with your organization is only the beginning of your search for new donors. The next step is to cultivate them, or to find ways to bring them closer to your organization. In these times of economic difficulty, cultivation is one area of campaign activity that remains completely under your control and that of your campaign leaders. It deserves careful analysis and attention as you move to put your campaign back on the track to success.

The definition of cultivation is clear: It is a series of steps, often increasing in their level of personalization and involvement, that bring the prospect closer to making a financial investment in the institution.

What is often not clear is how much cultivation it takes to convince a prospect to make a gift, or how much time should pass in the cultivation of a prospect, or even what steps constitute cultivation within a particular organization. While there are individual differences in the way each prospect responds to cultivation, it is possible to create a cultivation pattern, or a series of parallel steps, for all major prospects in the campaign.

Some campaigns pay too little attention to cultivation. This results in rushing the prospect to the point of solicitation, which usually results in a smaller gift or no gift at all. Some campaigns cultivate a prospect for years before anyone asks for a gift. We have literally seen prospects die after years of cultivation without any ask having been made. Neither of these scenarios is healthy for a capital campaign on the rocks.

Step back and consider what activities will bring prospects closer to understanding and appreciating the needs of your organization. Cultivation should encourage the development of strong personal relationships between the prospect and the leaders or volunteers of the nonprofit. Think about the answers to these kinds of questions:

- How can someone become more engaged in the work of our organization?
- What "touch points," or emotional ties, can be made with a prospect fairly easily?
- How can our prospects gain a sense of trust in our finances and our leadership?
- What kind of events do our prospects attend in our community?
- How can our prospects get a sense of the urgency of our campaign?

Cultivation activities will differ from city to city and from one institution to another. Decisions about cultivation should be made after a full discussion with your campaign leaders and campaign committee. Cultivation activity is an area where you will improve your outcomes by seeking input from volunteers who are already familiar with your organization and your community.

For example, let us say that after a bout of research, you have identified 10 family foundations, all located in your region, that you think could be viewed as new prospects for your campaign. Focus on two or three activities that your organization could provide to bring their trustees closer to the people and the work of your nonprofit. See Exhibit 6.4 for ideas about how to organize these activities into a cultivation continuum.

EXHIBIT 6.4

Suggested Cultivation Steps for Approaching Local Family Foundations

1. Ask your campaign committee to review a list of all the trustees of all the foundations. If personal connections do surface, use that volunteer as your contact with the foundation for all the activities outlined here.

2. Send each foundation director an invitation for them and their trustees to tour your site and see firsthand what services you provide in the community. Have them meet successful graduates of your programs. Don't ask for money—just use the visit to get to know each other.

3. Invite the foundation trustees (try to do no more than eight at one time) to a small, intimate dinner at the home of one of your campaign leaders. Bring the Executive Director/CEO to talk about programs and needs, but don't ask for money. Use the time to build a personal relationship with each trustee.

4. Send a volunteer and/or staff member to call on each foundation to begin a conversation about giving to the campaign. Educate them specifically about your campaign, your needs, and the timetable. Ask open-ended questions like, "What is the dollar range of giving we could apply for?" and, "What does your foundation expect in terms of recognition for a gift?" Use the time to educate, but also bring back information that can be used to write a proposal.

5. Write the proposal. After the proposal is sent, ask one of your campaign volunteers who has met the foundation's trustees to make a phone call. Have the volunteer use the call to remind the trustee of their personal interest in the gift, and ask the trustee to look out for your proposal. (Your volunteer can offer to have the trustee call if any questions arise during the review of the proposal.)

KEY CONCEPT

The goal of cultivation is to build a personal relationship and an affinity with your organization among people of means who will then make a decision to invest in meeting your needs.

Cultivation, by definition, is not a one-time experience with your organization. Completing three or four cultivation steps with a prospect takes time. Experience shows that the cultivation time for a brand-new prospect may take anywhere from 6 to 18 months. Taking these steps will ensure, however, that your ask will not fall on deaf ears.

After appropriate cultivation, the prospects will understand your mission, know your leadership, and have a better feeling for your needs. Taking the extra time to make these steps happen—instead of just popping off a proposal to the nearest foundation office—is what makes the difference between a successful solicitation and one that gets turned down on arrival.

Cultivating Out of Town Prospects

Most of the activities that fundraisers tend to think of as cultivation steps are better suited for prospects who live within their immediate region. How can campaigns successfully cultivate prospects who are far away? While this type of prospect may require some extra communication strategies, there are always

ways to make people feel at home. In fact, it is easier now than ever before to keep people in your fold. (See Exhibit 6.5).

EXHIBIT 6.5

Examples of Prospect Cultivation Activities

- Invite a prospect to tour your facility; show them a video, have them meet with users of your services.

- Take a prospect to lunch with a small campaign team; use one or two volunteers and one staff member (or the Executive Director/CEO) for each prospect.

- Hold a series of small, intimate dinners in the homes of campaign volunteers or leaders of the organization. Use the time to create personal connections and educate them about your needs, but don't ask.

- Hold a large cocktail style reception at your facility. Show the video, talk about campaign needs, and tell them someone will be calling on them to follow up.

- Identify easy ways for campaign prospects to volunteer for your organization.

- Have a campaign volunteer call a prospect and offer to accompany them to an event hosted by your organization, but not a fundraising event.

- Give an award or honor to a special prospect at an event.

- Write an article about something special that ties a prospect to your organization.

- Ask the prospect to help your campaign in some way, for instance, by participating in a feasibility study.

- Ask the prospect for advice. It's always flattering to the person being asked.

- Ask the prospect to help you identify other donors, and explain through that process how urgent your needs are.

- Invite the prospect on a trip or visit related to your mutual interests (e.g., tour an out-of-town art museum with art prospects).

- **And don't forget, at the end of the cultivation process, someone must ask!**

TIPS AND TECHNIQUES

Cultivation Ideas for Prospects Who Live Far Afield

- Send out a monthly newsletter or e-mail blast.
- Travel to key cities to visit prospects at least once a year. During an active campaign period, double up to twice a year or more.
- Plan events in key cities and include prospects in those cities. Make sure they are aware of everything your organization does in their region.
- Create a calendar tickler system to make a phone call or send an e-mail to each prospect on your list once a month or once a quarter.
- Send prospects a regular newsletter or annual report, but attach a little personal note to it, just to show your interest in them.
- Invite prospects to come to your organization's home city for a signature event; this could be a kickoff, a reunion, or a special campaign dinner.

Making Asks that Succeed

Turning around a campaign requires more than finding and cultivating a new cadre of prospects. Someone in your campaign must develop an expertise in asking and closing gifts, and it would be better if there were more than one person with this skill!

Training volunteers, management, and advancement staff on how to ask for and close a gift is not easy. This is the kind of skill that comes with practice. There are even executive directors and CEOs who can't close a gift to save their organization. What to do?

The first step toward success is to identify several key closers. These people can be selected from your available cohort of volunteers and staff (even the CEO can become a gift closer). There are professional seminars that offer training on how to ask for and close gifts. You might want to review the offerings from professional organizations such as CASE, AAM, and AFP. Consider hiring a local fundraising consultant to run a half-day training exercise with your group. When in doubt, use the tried and true method of running a series of role-playing exercises with your group members. Have them take turns between role-playing the donor and the solicitor to understand the dynamics.

Our preferred method of training volunteers and staff is to pair them up and send them on real calls with an experienced campaign volunteer. There is no substitute for the nuances and interpersonal dynamics of a real call on a real prospect, and the experienced one can show the trainee how it is done. After a few calls, switch teams and let the experienced volunteer train someone new to keep things fresh.

When to Ask

One of the hardest judgments to make regarding a prospect is knowing when to ask for the gift. There are some tried and true techniques to use at this stage, but you and your volunteers may have to come up with a technique that works for you. Experience is a plus at this point in the process, because experienced campaign volunteers seem to develop an intuitive sense about when a prospect is ready.

We believe that more campaigns err on the side of waiting too long to ask than the other way around. On the other hand, it is very important, given the weak economy, to give prospects time to get to know you. They may be giving less overall, so you want to be high on their list of giving priorities.

Here are some strategies to help you decide when to make the ask.

The Money Talk

Some organizations are more oriented toward using advancement staff in the solicitation of gifts, and some are more comfortable using volunteers. Probably the best idea is to combine them in a team format, so that the strengths of one side can support the strengths of the other side. This strategy, which I call the *money talk*, is best used by the staff, and should take place before the solicitation call.

The money talk is an off-the-record conversation between the advancement staff member and a prospect about the pending solicitation call. The goal for the staff member is to gain intelligence on the readiness of the prospect, how much he is expecting to be asked for, and what his current attitude is regarding making a contribution.

The idea is that the prospect—without fear of being pressured—will informally let the staff know his preferences concerning the pending solicitation. All parties involved expect the information gleaned to be treated confidentially, but the prospect also expects his solicitors to understand his position, that is, he knows that the information will be shared with them before the solicitation call. Some prospects will be very specific and even tell you who should call on them! Listen well and put what they say to good use.

Ask the Prospect for Guidance

In these more difficult times, there may be good reason for a prospect to drag his heels on making a gift. Sometimes the best idea is just to let the prospect guide you in setting the appropriate timing for a solicitation. Just as with the money talk, a staff member or volunteer close to the prospect should ask for her advice.

The conversation can be fairly direct, and could go something like this:

Muffy, as you know, we are in a capital campaign to build our new facility. This is very important to the future of our organization. I know you understand our needs now that you have seen some of the results of our past work. We would love to ask you to help us by making a gift. When do you think is a good time for us to call on you?

Most prospects, when faced with a direct question like this one, will give a direct answer. You should be able to ascertain the best timing for the ask from their response. If they ask for more time, give it to them. Many individuals (and foundations) are still trying to adjust to the reduced value of their assets going forward, and they need to decide how much they can afford to give. If it takes more time to move a prospect from a gift of $25,000 to a gift of $250,000, the extra time is worth it.

Getting to the Ask

Solicitation calls can be challenging but are often also fun and rewarding. Think about them as if you were approaching a play in which some characters already know their lines, and others have to make up their responses as the script unfolds. It is a bit like improvisational drama. The more you practice, the better you get; and the same is true for your CEO and your campaign volunteers.

Exhibit 6.6 identifies some issues to consider as you are setting up the solicitation call. Perhaps the most important point is who should go on the ask. The maximum size of the team that makes the call should be three people. If the solicitation team is too large, the prospect could feel threatened or pressured, which is less likely to result in the very best gift the prospect could make.

KEY CONCEPT

Keep the solicitation team to a maximum of three people, and always include the person in the organization who is the closest to the prospect on the call.

EXHIBIT 6.6

Issues to Consider Ahead of a Solicitation Call

1. **Who should go on the call?** Keep the team down to two or three people and include the person in the organization who is closest to the prospect.

2. **How should the call be organized?** Offer the prospect several dates and times that have already been cleared with your team in advance.

3. **Where should the call take place?** Offer to meet the prospect any place of her choosing (within reason). Try to select a place that is both private and quiet. Homes, board rooms, conference rooms, and quiet restaurants are fine. Busy coffee shops, airports, and offices provide too much distraction and noise.

4. **Who should set up the meeting?** Many advancement staff members prefer to make this call for themselves. Use an administrative assistant only if she is going to be speaking to the prospect's administrative assistant. If the prospect is very important and likely to prove difficult, have a volunteer or peer make the appointment.

5. **Should you tell the prospect that you are coming to ask for money?** Probably yes, if she asks. Probably no, if she doesn't ask. This may depend on who is doing the calling (an administrative assistant calling on your behalf should not offer this information to the prospect). Emphasize that a personal visit is important and tell her that you are coming to talk about her support. Do not let the prospect push you into making the ask on the phone!

6. **How should you prepare?** At the very least, prepare an outline with pointers for what each of the team members will say and in what order they will speak. If the call is an important one, write out a script in advance. If it's a really important call, or if the team hasn't worked together before, meet in advance with the whole team and practice some responses to possible questions. Become familiar with the prospect's giving record to your organization before going on the call.

7. **What should you bring?** We know experienced solicitors who bring nothing but their own wits and passion for the organization. Most of us need something additional to fall back on, which could be a packet with a proposal, or just a list of naming and recognition opportunities. Consider bringing a gift table, filled in to show what has been raised to date and what is needed. Determine how well the prospect has been cultivated. If she already has a campaign brochure, don't bring a second one. If the prospect asks for something you didn't bring, that gives you a good opportunity to follow up later. Don't bring too much!

The solicitation call for a gift of $5,000 or more should almost always be made in person. One campaign had success in asking for and closing a six-figure gift with a prospect by e-mail, but that is the exception that proves the rule. In that case, the prospect was someone who was heavily cultivated, had signaled he was ready to make a gift, and who worked in an Internet company. Don't try an e-mail solicitation for a major gift with most prospects!

There are good reasons to pair a volunteer with a staff member on your solicitation team. Staff members have more experience talking about specific aspects of pledges, recognition, and project details. Advancement staff who ask all the time are usually quicker to move to the ask and can close the gift more easily than volunteers, who may only do this two or three times a year. Staff also are better at reporting back exactly what happened on the call, which can assist the organization with record keeping, follow-up, and writing a proposal (if one is needed).

Volunteers have their own strengths. Many of them are donors themselves (most campaigners only bring volunteers who are current donors with them on calls) and can talk about the experience of giving from the donor perspective. Some may be social peers or old friends of the prospects, which can aid in closing the gift. Volunteers are more likely to be passionate, to sway the donor to give at the same level they have given and can provide peer pressure to help close the gift.

IN THE REAL WORLD

What Is the Best Setting for an Ask?

The university president had arranged to meet a prospect from out of town at a downtown luxury hotel for breakfast. The prospect was staying in that hotel, so it seemed a natural choice. When they got there at 8:00 A.M. the restaurant was unaccountably closed. They walked next door to a Wendy's and the president asked for $1 million over a fast-food breakfast. The donor seemed amused at the setting, congratulated the president on saving some money over the breakfast, and agreed to the gift right then and there.

Making the Ask: Five Basic Steps

Once the team has been assembled, prepared, and is ready to meet with the prospect, there are five basic steps to making a solicitation call. These steps should not be rushed or skipped if the solicitation is done well. In these difficult times, it is hard enough to bring a prospect to the point of a solicitation, so make sure the process is carried out in the very best possible manner.

If necessary, practice ahead of time with the team. The staff should always prepare an outline for each team member with information about the prospect, his giving history to the organization, the ask amount, and other details of the call, such as who will say what and the major points to cover. We strongly recommend making specific assignments to the team ahead of time for who will handle which portion of the call, so that there are no misunderstandings during the meeting. Little should be left to chance.

Step 1: Greetings and Introductions

The first five minutes or so of the call should be spent making everyone comfortable, getting water or coffee, making small talk, and then moving to introduce everyone on the team. Make sure that the donor—and everyone present—understands who each player in the group is. Don't waste too much time at this stage, as you may need extra time later in the call. Always ascertain how long the prospect has left his schedule open for the meeting so that you don't run out of time at the end, when important details need to be settled.

Identify one person on the team who will take charge of the transition, moving the conversation into the business portion of the meeting, by saying something like this:

Now, Bill, as you know, we are all here to talk about the museum. Let's begin with some facts about its needs. Mary, can you fill us in on where we are with the campaign?

Step 2: Presenting the Need

If the prospect has been well cultivated, presenting the need will include a summary of the organization's current situation, its future plans, how the needs have been identified, and what the prospect's gift will contribute toward remedying the need. This can be done in about 10 to 15 minutes, depending on the extent of knowledge that the prospect already has attained. Even with prospects who are close to the organization, don't skip this step. This is the segment of the conversation that gives substance to the pending ask by tying the money to the needs.

In a strong ask, with a prospect who has been well cultivated, we predict that the gift will easily follow the conversation about the need. In most cases the prospect is already in alignment with the needs and the work of the organization, or the conversation wouldn't have gotten to this point.

If the need is presented correctly, what you want the prospect to say is: "What can I do to help?"

This is the step where the solicitors' passion for the cause will come into play. Creating an emotional tie with the prospective donor is an important element of fundraising and is sometimes overlooked in the actual solicitation meeting. Pictures, stories, videos, PowerPoint presentations, and brochures can all be used at this point. Pick carefully among the options available and make sure the supporting documentation tells the story that you want told. Remember that a picture is worth a thousand words!

These options should be discussed and prepared ahead of the call. If you are using an electronic format, make sure that you have access to the appropriate equipment in the place where the meeting is taking place. It's embarrassing to have to stop at this point to get the PowerPoint working, and it interrupts the momentum of the meeting.

Presenting your campaign needs can be accomplished through using a variety of formats during the meeting:

- One of the team members can tell a short personal story about her experience with the work of the organization.

- Play a short video that evokes the experiences of people who have used the services of the organization.

- Display still photos arranged in a photo book to illustrate a story or to show off the plans for a new facility.

- Show a PowerPoint presentation about a new facility.

- Walk the prospect through a campaign brochure that illustrates the needs.

- Bring along blueprints and an artist's rendering if the ask is for a new facility.

Make sure that everything your team presents is in good taste. Images of pathetic victims don't need to be overdone or elaborated on. Short and sweet is the order of the day for the solicitation meeting. A 3- to 4-minute video can pack more punch than a drawn-out 15-minute slide presentation. Train your team to be genuine, brief, and specific: The prospect should fully understand what project she is being asked to give to, what the gift will do for the organization, and why the gift is urgent.

Step 3: Making the Ask

Making the ask is the part of the solicitation call that team members often dread the most. There is really no reason for this dread. The prospect should be ready by this point; she has been cultivated, educated, and understands the need and urgency of the cause. What remains is to not only confirm her financial support, but to confirm at what level she will make her gift.

KEY CONCEPT

In order to get the best results from a personal solicitation call, the ask must include a dollar figure.

An ask has not been made if a dollar figure isn't named. Sometimes the solicitor is nervous about naming an amount and fudges the ask, blending it into a general request for support. This is not a personal solicitation! Asking requires discipline, and the discipline of asking for a specific amount will help guide the prospect toward a gift at the level that the institution expects and needs.

Making the ask at a specific dollar level doesn't mean that the donor and the team have to settle immediately on the final amount of the gift. Reaching the dollar figure of the final gift is a negotiating process, and this negotiation process will follow the ask. Negotiation may even take several steps beyond this meeting. The purpose of making the ask at a specific amount is to convey several messages to the donor:

- It tells the donor that the organization is taking her involvement, her gift, and her capacity to make a gift seriously.

- It tells her how much the organization needs from her.

- It tells her what the organization thinks she is capable of giving (rightly or wrongly).

- It gives her a figure to reference during the negotiation stage of the meeting.

- It allows the solicitation team to link the ask amount to a specific recognition opportunity.

TIPS AND TECHNIQUES

Making the Ask Should Be for a Specific Dollar Amount and Should Be Linked to the Recognition That Accompanies a Gift at That Level

Here are three examples:

1 We would like to ask you to make a $100,000 gift to the campaign for the new Education Center. A gift at this level would allow you to name the new conference room in the center "The Jones Family Conference Center," or another name that you choose.

2 We are here to ask you to consider a gift of $1.5 million to endow the position of the executive director of the Children's Museum. This gift would allow the museum to link your family's name permanently with the executive director's position. For instance, the position could be known as the "Jones Family Executive Director" on all the museum's stationery, announcements, and publications.

③ We would like you to consider joining us at the $20,000 level. This leadership level allows you to receive several benefits, including having your name listed as a lead sponsor in our program. Your family will also be invited to the private preview event to meet our guest star before the program.

Note that the ask does not necessarily have to include a time period for the gift, nor does it indicate how or with what assets the gift will be made. In most cases, the pledge period and asset issues are points that are better saved for the negotiation phase. This allows for a more graceful fallback position for the team and the donor if she is unable or unwilling to make the gift at the level for which she was asked.

IN THE REAL WORLD

The advancement VP took a foundation trustee and her attorney out to a fancy dinner at a restaurant that featured a famous chef (they were from out of town). The restaurant was so noisy that she could hardly hear a thing they said during the entire dinner conversation. At the critical point, the foundation trustee leaned over and said, "We would like to do mmmph (something inaudible) for you." The VP completely missed the dollar figure and had to ask for a repeat when they finally got outside an hour later. "I said we would do $2 to 3 million!" was the answer—not something you would want to miss!

There always exists a possibility that the donor will want to make a large cash gift up front, and adding a pledge period to the ask takes that potential away from her. Making the assumption that the gift will have to be pledged over a number of years could cheat the organization out of a larger, present-value gift.

As the development truism goes, after the ask is made, the solicitor should remain silent. The prospective donor needs time to process the ask, time to consider the amount, and time to formulate an appropriate response. Train your solicitors to make the ask and then say nothing until the donor speaks, no matter how awkward the silence becomes! We tell our team members to count to 10 slowly, and bite their tongues if need be. The old rule of negotiation goes that after the ask, he who speaks first, loses. We do not hold with the concept that making a gift is losing, but the point is clear—let the donor respond first.

TIPS AND TECHNIQUES

Two Techniques for Making the Ask

❶ The Volunteer Ask. Have a team member who has already made a gift near, at, or above the level that you are asking the donor for make the ask. This ask has to be planned out in advance by including the right volunteer on the team and making sure that he is ready to name the amount of his gift.

The volunteer ask goes like this:

Bob, I know you understand how important this project is to our city and our region. I have already made a commitment myself of $100,000 to the campaign. We are hoping that you will consider a gift at the same level, $100,000, to name the new conference room in the Education Center.

❷ The Gift Table Ask. Make the ask using a handout that shows the gift table of all gifts that have been made but that also shows the gifts that are needed at each level (see Exhibit 6.7).

The gift table ask goes like this:

Bob, you can see from this table that we only have one donor in at the $20,000 level, and we need at least two to make this program successful. I hope that you will consider helping us achieve our goal by making a leadership commitment at this level. Your $20,000 will allow us to list you as a major sponsor on the program and the invitation to the program.

Step 4: Negotiating the Gift

This step usually starts with some questions from the donor. Be sure to have answers to questions like those listed below, and role play questions with your team members ahead of time if they are new to the solicitation process. Try

EXHIBIT 6.7

Sample Handout for Gift Table Ask (Total Campaign Goal is $185,000)

Gift Level	# Donors	# Raised	# Needed	$ Raised	$ Needed
$20,000	2	1	1	$ 20,000	$20,000
$10,000	6	4	2	$ 40,000	$20,000
$ 5,000	12	6	6	$ 30,000	$30,000
$ 1,000	25	20	5	$ 20,000	$ 5,000
Totals	**45**	**31**	**14**	**$110,000**	**$75,000**

to answer everything fully and honestly. If there is some detail that you can't respond to on the spot, offer to get the answer and call the donor back later. Following up on the donor's concerns is an important element in closing the gift, so make sure it isn't overlooked.

Here are some examples of typical questions (and suggested answers) that a prospective donor could ask at this point in the meeting:

Donor: I can't do that size gift all at once. What is the pledge period for the campaign?

Team member: We need to break ground on the new building by next January. We are requesting that donors make three-year pledges so that we can get the money in hand for construction as soon as possible.

Donor: I'm not sure what your policy is on endowment payout. Can you tell me more about how the endowment is invested, how it has weathered the current economy, and what the payout level would be?

Team member: Our endowment has weathered the storm pretty well. As you know, we invest with the Jones Company, which has guided us fairly conservatively. Over the past 10 years before the current market troubles we have averaged a 12 percent return.

While the market has dropped over 30 percent since last October, our endowment has only dropped 15 percent. As you know, this is a long-term gift and the endowment will rise as the market comes back. The board is about to have a finance committee meeting to discuss the endowment payout for the next year. If you would like, I can have Suzy Savings, our chief financial officer, call you after that meeting.

Donor: I would like to give $20,000 as a sponsor, but my wife needs to be included in the decision. I need to talk to her and get back to you. Can you give me some time for that?

Team member: Sure, we would be glad to come back and speak to you and your wife together if that would be helpful. We are going to press with the program and invitation in two weeks. Do you think you could reach a decision by then so that we can include your name on the invitation?

Negotiating the Gift Amount

During the negotiation phase, the donor may substitute a smaller number. There are several responses that might help your team to respond to this appropriately. Your team's choice of responses will depend on how optimistic they are about the donor's interest in the project, how soon they expect the economy to rebound, and how they assess the giving capability of the donor.

Donor: Well, I'd like to do $100,000 for the conference room, but given the economy and the decline in my business, I really think all we can do is $25,000. What are the recognition options for a gift of that size?

Team member: (choice one, close the gift): Thanks, we appreciate your generous offer of $25,000. You can name the Jones Family Classroom for a gift of this amount, and we will show you a building layout so you can select a classroom of your choice.

Team member: (choice two: keep the gift size open): Thank you, we are grateful for your offer, but we have so few donors like you who might be able to make the gift for that conference room. Do you think that your family might be willing to think about the $100,000 if it were spread over a five-year pledge? That would only amount to $20,000 per year.

Note that the donor had offered $25,000 without a time frame; this counter-offer actually lowers the annual gift amount to $20,000/year if the donor meant to pay the $25,000 all in one year.

Step 5: Closing the Gift

After all the questions are answered, it is time to close the gift. Make sure that one team member has been assigned to do this important task. It does not have to be the same team member who presented the needs or who made the ask. Many teams use volunteers to summarize the case and make the ask, then a staff member or the CEO steps in to close the gift.

If a gift has been promised, a good close repeats the ask amount, the timing, and the particulars of the gift. The close also sets a specific time and date for a next action. For example:

Closing statement from the CEO: Thank you so much, Bob. As I understand it, you are pledging to give us $100,000 from your family foundation over five years to name the conference room, with the first payment to come before December 30. I can't tell you how much this means to us. I will have my staff send you a pledge letter to sign within the next three days. Why don't you and your wife let us know how you want the conference room named? Do you want the letter to come to your house or to the foundation address?

If there has been no resolution, it is even more critical to set a specific next step, preferably one that includes an action step with a date attached:

Closing statement from a campaign volunteer: Thanks for having us here, Bob. We hope you realize the importance of this request to our programs. We would love to invite you and your wife over to see the site and review the blueprints with our architect. I think that would help to answer some of your questions about the site and use of the conference room. Do you think we could set that meeting up for next week?

How does Tuesday look?

Examples of Closing Statements

- *Thanks, Mary. We will get back to you by Friday on that recognition question. Once it has been answered, can I call you about your gift? How does early next week look on your calendar?*

- *Thanks, Joe. We share your concern about the incorrect spelling of your name in last year's program. I am sure it was just a clerical error. Can we assure you that you will get to see the program proof before it goes to print this year? We want you to be happy with the way you are recognized. I would like to call you next Wednesday to follow up after you have more time to think about this.*

- *Janet, you have always been so generous to us. Our donor list goes into print December 1. Can we touch base with you before then to make sure that your name and gift are on the list? We don't want to miss recognizing you for all your help. Do you think you could have a response for us by November 15?*

- *Johnnie, I can fully understand that this is a family decision. Do you think that you can meet with your sons and make a commitment before we break ground for the building in January? We really want your gift to be recognized during that ceremony. How about if we give the kids a tour of the site the next time they are in town? Is that going to be at Christmas?*

After the Call Is Completed

Give the team a few minutes to wind down and identify a team member who will write up some notes on what happened during the meeting. This is another reason to have a staff member on the call, because the records will often be kept better if a staff member prepares them. It is very important to write down the next steps, assign them, and have someone follow up to make sure they are followed. If a proposal must be written, or a pledge letter prepared, be sure to tell the staff all they need to know to handle it correctly. Leaving off the pledge period, getting the amount wrong, or identifying the wrong project is a gift killer!

Don't forget to write or e-mail a thank-you note to the donor right away, even if the gift hasn't been promised at the meeting. You want to keep the prospect on your side no matter how tough the call actually was. The prospect who airs a grievance during a solicitation call can turn into a loyal friend and donor if the grievance is handled correctly. The worst attitude to encounter with a prospective donor is lassitude or disinterest. The prospect who shows concern at how she has been treated or anger at something the organization has done is indicating interest by means of her emotion. Fix the problem and she could still deliver on the gift.

It used to be a development axiom that you could never ask for too much. The new economy has thrown that rule out the window. Ask for a reasonable amount based on the prospect's past giving, known assets, and gift amounts to other organizations. Being greedy has gone out of fashion.

Summary

Your campaign could probably make use of additional prospects. Because prospect research methods have improved exponentially with Internet search capabilities, you should consider using an electronic prospect research firm to help you identify and prioritize your top prospects.

Electronic prospect screening should be augmented by the work of a prospect researcher who can add personal information about the prospect's giving interests and any connections and ties to your organization. Formal screening and rating programs as well as ongoing prospect list review with volunteers, are also tried and true methods for expanding prospect lists.

Once the prospect list is developed, plan a series of cultivation events or personal contacts with each of your prospects so that they become more knowledgeable about your organization. Engaging prospects in the work of your nonprofit through volunteer service is often a productive way to encourage new donations. Think about cultivation as a series of contacts that will produce a stronger relationship with the prospect within a set time period.

Finally, plan the solicitation process with care. Select the right team, the right setting, and assign roles ahead of time to make your team as effective as possible. Always ask for a specific amount. Don't forget to use some of the closing techniques discussed in this chapter to make sure that the solicitation call actually results in a gift to your organization. Training workshops, role playing, and making calls with a practiced solicitor are all ways to help your team become skilled at making effective solicitations.

CHAPTER 7

Communicate More Effectively to Attract Additional Support

After reading this chapter you will be able to:

- Sharpen your case to stand out in the crowd.
- Create materials that motivate donors.
- Write stronger proposals.

Communicate to Attract Support

When money is tight and the competition for scarce resources has heated up, it is more important than ever to distinguish your campaign with a strong communications program and outstanding campaign materials. This may require a review of marketing and communication strategies across your organization.

You will most likely need to sharpen your case for support. "Sharpening the case" is the term used for focusing the message of why a donor should give to your organization and communicating that message succinctly through a variety of media to prospective donors.

Review Marketing and Communication Strategies

Marketing decisions, communication methods, messages, web sites, and printed materials are all important components of campaign outreach. They can also drive up the costs of fundraising. As part of your campaign analysis, do an unofficial communications audit. This means pulling out copies of all the printed information that your prospects would have received since the campaign began.

Be sure to identify all regular institutional mailings such as bills, pledge reminders, program newsletters, announcements, invitations, and magazines, even if they are not produced through the advancement office. Don't forget to review electronic communication and web sites. You will want to assess all the various communication factors that could influence prospects to form an opinion about the work your organization is involved in, recent accomplishments, and institutional needs.

Evaluate materials and messaging on the following factors:

- Do they provide a clear and compelling explanation of the organization's needs?

- Do they communicate key accomplishments effectively?

- Do they create a strong emotional bond between the reader and the organization?

- Do they represent the organization accurately, honestly, and on a timely basis?

- Do they provide a basic continuity of look and feel that cuts across departmental boundaries?

- Is the cost reasonable within the context of the needs and goals of the organization?

As you evaluate the materials, think about ways that messages and materials could be revised to support your campaign communication needs. Messaging could be integrated so that when other departments produce printed materials, they focus on the same needs that the campaign is raising funds for. If donors are receiving conflicting messages about needs from different areas in the organization, then the overall institutional communication plan needs streamlining.

It is possible to reach across institutional barriers and create broad communication strategies for an organization. Work with colleagues to maximize the impact that all printed and electronic materials deliver. If you are in a capital campaign for a new building, then set an organizational priority on stories that focus on the need for more space. The newsletter produced for volunteers might illustrate crowded conditions in the current facility, while the web site is used to highlight a beautiful rendering of the new facility. Use the monthly magazine or newsletter to describe the programs that the new facility will make possible.

Think about ways to make do with fewer printed materials and add more electronic communication and media. There are three reasons for this switch: you will save on printing costs, you will save on mailing costs, and your organization will appear to be more up-to-date to your audience. Many nonprofits now produce their annual reports online. Determine that your organization will be ahead of the curve in using new communication methods rather than behind it.

 IN THE REAL WORLD

Many nonprofits now publish their annual reports and newsletters online. One secondary school mailed out a postcard to all its constituents, alerting them to the decision to publish its annual report online. The postcard gave the URL for the online report and also offered a printed version to anyone who requested one. Interested parties were asked to call a number on campus to request a hard copy. Fewer than 5 percent of their constituents did so, saving the school over $40,000 in printing and mailing costs.

Sharpen Your Case to Stand Out

Focus Communication on One or Two Overriding Themes

Marketing experts working with for-profit companies help them to determine their business focus and create a messaging plan based on that focus. The same techniques can work in the nonprofit sector.

Ask this simple question about your organization: *What business are you in?* The answer(s) will help you learn to portray your organization in a light that attracts additional donor support. The best answer (at least for advancement purposes) is not always as clear and obvious as it might seem.

Consider these two examples:

1. *The Art Museum*

   An art museum conducted a capital campaign to build a new addition. The goal was to expand the amount of exhibition space so that the museum could bring in larger traveling blockbuster shows, which would draw crowds from across the region.

   What business was the museum in? Most people would probably answer "the arts." The museum's leaders decided to undertake some research to help them identify a case that could provide a sense of urgency and need across different facets of their community.

   The museum needed to expand beyond its traditional base, which was composed of a small circle of older, wealthy art collectors. After holding community focus groups and conducting a feasibility study, the leaders made a decision that they would market their needs by focusing on new areas of emphasis.

   Ultimately they decided on these themes for making their case:

   - Expanding programs in K–12 arts education.

   - Economic development through cultural tourism.

   Choosing the first theme, education, allowed them to approach new prospects who were interested in educational outreach and arts education.

Their plans to increase their outreach to K–12 schools during large exhibitions were especially attractive to local and national foundations.

Selecting the second focus area, economic development through cultural tourism, gave the museum an opportunity to make its case to local and regional corporations, including those that worked with the tourist industry in their region. They were able to broaden their prospect list to include tourism-based enterprises like hotels and shopping centers.

Their new market position also allowed them to make a strong argument to their city and state governments that they were an important component of their region's plan for economic growth. This led to additional public funds in support of their campaign efforts.

2. *The Jazz Summer Camp*

A summer camp offered high quality but inexpensive professional training and workshops in jazz to local youngsters who showed promise in music. After 10 years of operations on a shoestring budget, the school director wanted to expand the camp's financial resources beyond a few well-known backers.

What business was the camp in? Most of the board members and faculty would have responded "education" or perhaps "music education." They decided to meet with a consultant for a board retreat to refocus their marketing and communication strategy with the goal of reaching a wider base of potential supporters in their community and nationally.

During the retreat, many teachers spoke passionately about their experiences with helping young minority students from low-income families discover and develop their musical talents. They felt that many of these children might have been lost to the dangerous street culture of their neighborhoods without the intervention of the summer camp.

Talking about the student stories led to the group adopting the theme of "Saving Lives through Music." This is a case that could be illustrated with the poignant stories and photos of young people who had been given the support and skills necessary to overcome educational deficiencies and a lack of opportunity in their everyday lives. By developing this theme in its materials, the group could make its case to a broad group of prospective donors who would feel an emotional tie to the camp's work.

Basic Elements of the Case

Sharpening the case is a matter of reassessing the case that has been developed for your campaign to see if it includes all six of the basic case elements in Exhibit 7.1. It is possible that your case has been made too broadly, or that it doesn't appeal directly to the emotions. In many campaigns the case lacks urgency. It is important to distinguish why someone needs to give *now* in order to convince donors that your organizational needs have priority over other causes they may consider giving to.

Exhibit 7.1 identifies the basic elements for making a strong case. Let us look at each of them in more detail.

The first component is to link the case to the organization's mission, services, and goals. This is the element that gives the case its legitimacy; the campaign must derive its urgency, its appeal, and its emotional core from the real

---

EXHIBIT 7.1

Six Elements for Making a Strong Case

There are six elements for making a strong case for support for your campaign:

1. The case must legitimately be linked to the mission, services, and goals of the organization.
2. The case must explain the nature of the need and why it is important.
3. The case must be able to develop an emotional tie between the prospect and the work of the organization.
4. The case must show the urgency of the need.
5. The case must be comprehensible to the general public.
6. The case must be able to be communicated easily by a broad base of supporters and through a variety of printed and electronic media.

---

work of the organization. A university, for instance, would always want to tie its case back to higher education. Following this precept will help the organization avoid any potential dissonance between its marketing of its needs and the reality of its needs.

The second element means that the case must be tied in some way to the needs of the campaign. If a university needs more scholarship funds, for instance, then in its campaign case it will explain the growing financial challenges in middle class families, the heavy burden of student loans on a young graduate's career, and the lack of access to quality education among low income families.

Developing an emotional tie with the reader/recipient is the third element of making the case. This is often done through telling a story or showing a story. The case for university scholarships, for instance, can be a dry assessment of financial details and facts about financial aid, or it can be expressed through illustrated profiles of real students who are shown achieving real progress in their lives through the means of financial aid. A video that shows financial aid donors meeting aid recipients, for instance, can be a powerful motivator. The case must resonate emotionally with prospective donors in order to earn their support.

Many campaigns do not do enough to emphasize the urgency of their case for support. Urgency, or the need to act now, is a key component of campaign fundraising, because it presses donors to act now, rather than delaying. The campaign has a timetable and a goal that has to be reached within a set time-frame. Why? What will happen if the timetable is delayed or if the goal isn't met? The case must explain or at least imply that there are serious consequences if the campaign doesn't succeed, either to the organization or to the people that it provides services for. The case must show the donor why inaction is not an appropriate choice.

The last two requirements are that the case be comprehensible, and that it be easily communicated through different media. The best case is one that doesn't need a great deal of drawn out explanation. In working for the SPCA, for instance, most people understand—without reading a single page about it—that companion animals that are deserted, hurt, or lost need to go to a shelter.

The case should include an intellectual, rational component that can be explained logically, such as in a proposal, and that is supported by documentation and research on the need. However, the strongest case is one that is immediately accessible to a wide variety of people, in other words, most people will understand what it means and its importance without a great deal of persuasion.

The ability to develop the case for use in different media is critical because an effective campaign will need to use a variety of communication strategies to reach different audiences. The use of different media for presenting the case is discussed in the section that follows, but a strong and flexible case will be compelling whether it is presented through a printed brochure, pictures, video, or on the campaign web site.

Coordinate the Message across the Organization

In a time of shrinking budgets it is especially important to make sure that all communications sent out from the organization support the same messages. This way the organization will get more bang for the buck by reinforcing its selected themes across different audiences.

The themes developed for the campaign case should be shared with the entire organization and integrated into the materials produced by different departments. Some organizations formally centralize all their communications under one office in order to gain efficiency in their messaging and promotion. Others look for ways to weave the same important thematic elements into materials that are being produced by different departments.

Meet with your colleagues to discuss ways that messages that support your case can be shared across departmental boundaries. One group might want to revise the organizational web site, for instance, to feature profiles of people who have used your services to support the needs outlined in your case; others might be interested in highlighting programs in their area that contribute to the effectiveness of the case.

Bringing a group together across departmental and organizational boundaries to discuss effective communications strategies can be an effective way to combine messages, save money, and reach out to more people with a compelling argument about why they should support your needs.

Let us look at what kinds of communication materials are needed for getting your campaign back on track.

Creating Materials that Motivate Donors

Now that you know what message and themes you want to use to help develop your case, it is time to consider how to employ the various materials that can effectively communicate that message.

Most campaigns develop a printed brochure for use with prospects and volunteers that outlines their case for support. These campaign brochures, often called Case Statements, can range in complexity and length from an inexpensive trifold brochure, designed in-house, to a beautiful and expensive bound book in full color. If the budget allows for a printed brochure of several pages, there are some standard components that should be reviewed for inclusion (see Exhibit 7.2).

EXHIBIT 7.2

Components to Include in the Printed Campaign Brochure or Case Statement

- A letter from the Executive Director/CEO, or Campaign Chair.

- A brief mission statement.

- Abbreviated version of the case for the campaign (why should the donor give?).

- A description or list of the items that will be funded through the campaign.

- A statement or chart showing the campaign goal and timetable.

- A list of recognition opportunities with prices.

- A list of the names of the campaign committee members.

- A list of the names of the board members.

(Continued)

- Photographs that illustrate the needs or the work of the organization.

- If it is a capital campaign, floor plans or a rendering of the facility planned.

- A site plan if appropriate.

- Stories that support the case and create an emotional tie with the reader.

- Ways to give, including information about pledges and planned gifts.

- A statement about progress to date if the campaign is already under way.

Because each organization's needs for communicating with prospects will differ slightly, consider reviewing this list of Case Statement elements with your campaign volunteers to learn what they find works best with prospects. It is possible to produce a small, inexpensive printed brochure if most of the relevant information is available on the organization's web site, for instance. Or perhaps your group will want to create a series of small brochures or one-page campaign summaries that fit inside a printed folder.

In our experience, prospects are increasingly wary of slick, glossy brochures that cost a fortune. Most donors want their money to be spent on the work and needs of the nonprofit, and they realize that high overhead costs for design and printing only increase the cost of the campaign without solving any bigger issues.

Our advice is for clients to purchase inexpensive, custom-designed pocket folders that can be used to hold a wide assortment of information about the campaign. To make the folder more attractive, an organizational logo, title, or photo can be printed on the outside for branding purposes. Also consider using your campaign logo and colors on all the materials inside the folder to keep the look unified.

One of the advantages of the campaign folder over the campaign brochure is that it can be updated easily and inexpensively as information changes. We have worked with two large, national campaigns where big, expensive printed pieces designed by national communications consultants have been junked because the building plans, the goals, or the timetables became seriously outdated.

TIPS AND TECHNIQUES

Using the Pocket Folder

Use a custom printed pocket folder filled with materials that can be printed and updated in-house. This is less expensive and more flexible than printing a campaign brochure or case statement. Use campaign colors and logo on all materials to unify the look and feel of the package. Types of campaign materials that can be inserted (folders can be customized for each prospect) include:

- Short version of the campaign case statement.
- Photos of users of the organization's services.
- Floor plans and rendering of a new facility.
- Recognition opportunities and prices.
- Letter from the campaign chair(s).
- Quotes about the work of the organization from supporters.
- List of board members.
- List of campaign committee members.
- CD with campaign PowerPoint or video.
- Pledge card and return envelope.
- Mission and Vision statement.
- Written proposal for a gift.
- Budget for the project begin funded.
- Copies of PR articles about the project or organization.
- A business card of the staff member to contact for giving.

While a campaign folder may suit the needs of a smaller organization, many larger campaigns develop a variety of additional materials, both printed and electronic, to support their efforts. This is particularly true for multiyear campaigns, which must communicate with their donors and prospects over a long period of time.

A list of useful campaign materials that could be developed to mount a large, national capital campaign can be found in Exhibit 7.3.

EXHIBIT 7.3

Campaign Materials

A large national campaign might need some or all of these materials:

- Campaign Case Statement (main campaign brochure, used for calls).

- Smaller version of case statement (used for events, mailings).

- Pledge card and return envelope.

- Campaign video.

- Campaign web site (or dedicated pages on main web site).

- Campaign PowerPoint.

- Stationery with campaign letterhead, logo, and campaign committee list.

- Invitations for campaign events with logo.

- Campaign newsletter (monthly or quarterly).

- Volunteer handbook and volunteer job description.

- Signage or recognition plan.

- Ways to give: planned giving options and gift acceptance policy.

- Rendering and floor plans for a new facility.

- Proposal templates.

- Direct-mail solicitation pieces.

Note that you do not have to prepare all of these materials at the same time. Campaign year one, for instance, might introduce the Case Statement, the video and the volunteer handbook. In year two, the staff would add the ways of giving brochure and the smaller version of the case statement for use in events and mailings. Then by year three, when the campaign goes public, the organization beefs up its web site with a special campaign site to track progress, creates a monthly newsletter, and adds a campaign-focused direct mail piece.

Do not forget to use communications vehicles geared to other uses, like annual reports, alumni magazines, e-newsletters, and annual fund mailings, to support the case for the campaign. These ancillary pieces, often produced by staff members who are not associated with the campaign, can help to broaden the entire campaign communications effort when used effectively as a companion tool to materials that are produced for the campaign.

Schools and universities, for instance, often devote an entire issue of the alumni magazine to introducing the campaign, describing its needs, and making the case for why a graduate should give back to the institution. Future issues might contain a regular campaign update corner to keep readers informed on the progress of the campaign needs and goals.

There are some staff members (especially in educational circles) who strive to separate general communications with their constituents from fundraising asks. We can understand the reluctance (and share the goal) of not making every single mailing a solicitation; however, the better approach is to combine efforts strategically, so that messages from all divisions of the organization are synchronized in support of the advancement efforts.

One effective way to invigorate a stalled campaign is to create a campaign newsletter (see Exhibit 7.4 for ideas on content). Newsletters are especially effective as the campaign goes public and reaches out to broaden its funding base.

EXHIBIT 7.4

Quarterly Campaign Newsletter Options

Here are some options for what to include in a quarterly campaign newsletter:

- Letter from the chair of the campaign.

- Updated thermometer (a design element that fills up as the campaign dollars increase toward the goal).

- Photos from a recent campaign event.

- Announcement of new leadership gifts.

- Updates on the projects or buildings that are being funded by the campaign.

(Continued)

- Article on a planned giving technique.

- Article on endowment giving.

- Profile of a donor or volunteer.

- Profile of a recipient of services funded by the campaign.

The newsletter can be monthly or quarterly, depending on the resources available in staff, time, and budget. Some newsletters are now mailed purely as e-newsletters, which decreases their cost, but may not increase their readership. Do some testing with your audiences to determine if e-news alone is an appropriate way to transmit information to your constituents. It is all too easy for the recipient of electronic newsletters to hit the delete key.

TIPS AND TECHNIQUES

A Model for a Campaign Communications Plan on a Tight Budget

Materials needed for the quiet phase:

- Hold a contest to create a campaign logo (or ask a volunteer with design skills).
- Buy glossy, colored pocket folders at an office supply store; print campaign logo on a sticker and use on folder cover to brand the materials.
- Prepare all printed materials in-house; use logo to create campaign stationery.
- Stuff folder with case statement, copies of PR articles, quotes from supporters, floor plans, and photos.
- Prepare a PowerPoint with photos of the projects to be funded through the campaign; put on CD and include in folder.
- Prepare a strong proposal template to use with early prospects.

Materials needed for the public phase:

- Build a strong campaign web site, link to the home page of your organization's web site, include video and interactive elements.

- Create a quarterly e-newsletter to support campaign efforts.
- Create an inexpensive, trifold brochure to use as a direct mail piece to support campaign efforts.
- Develop an effective PR plan to reach out to new audiences.
- Plan a fun, inexpensive way to hold a campaign kickoff on-site, such as combining the kickoff with a fair, a homecoming celebration, or a community arts exhibition.
- Ask an older child or teen to design your event invitation to get a fresh, bold, and graphic look.

Using Electronic Media in Your Campaign

Consider how to best use electronic media to make your case effective and up to date. The message and the medium should be aligned. If your campaign is raising money for a science museum, use modern technology, such as a campaign web site with video downloads, to illustrate your needs. If your average prospect is young, hip, and carries a Blackberry, don't use only old-fashioned print media to get your message across.

If your average donor is a widow over the age of 65, design your materials with a large font size to make for easy reading. However, don't assume that older people don't use the Internet! Older folks have the time to browse and an interest in looking at the details of an organization before they make a gift. Make it easy for them by mailing your annual fund materials to all donors with the address of your campaign web site so that they can get a good look at what you offer.

Most organizations now have a web site, but few have really good web sites. A great web site should be built around the same themes that your case focuses on, have a look and design that is coordinated with the rest of the communication materials used by your organization, and be visually exciting. Campaign web sites now include interactive elements, including on-line giving, planned gift calculators, campaign blogs, e-mail contact information, and video snippets from recent events to make the site user-friendly and to keep donors returning to the site. (See Chapter 8 for a case study of a viral Internet campaign that was used to reach new donors in the public phase of a capital campaign.)

There are also many good ways to use a PowerPoint presentation in support of the campaign (see Exhibit 7.5). PowerPoint offers the capability of being easy to transport (by e-mail or on a disc), it is a technology familiar to and well accepted by prospects of all ages, and it can be inexpensively updated. PowerPoint presentations can contain video, music, photos, and other visual or aural elements that help to create an emotional tie with viewers.

Prepare for calls by supplying a laptop fitted out with a short PowerPoint program or video that your volunteers can use anytime with any prospect. A well designed PowerPoint or video can provide an inexpensive and powerful way to make the case in front of one person or a small group, such as a board of

---

EXHIBIT 7.5

Campaign PowerPoint Presentations

PowerPoint presentations can be used to make an effective case. Add music, sound, video, animation, and other elements to professionalize the presentation. Here is one basic sample outline for a campaign PowerPoint presentation:

Slide 1:   Logo and title of campaign.
Slide 2:   Brief summary of organization's history and mission (1).
Slide 3:   Brief summary of organization's history and mission (2).
Slide 4:   Identify need (1).
Slide 5:   Identify need (2).
Slide 6:   Show examples of service users to illustrate need (1).
Slide 7:   Show examples of service users (2).
Slide 8:   Identify costs and campaign goal.
Slide 9:   Show large gifts raised to date and total progress toward goal.
Slide 10: Review campaign timetable and urgency of need.
Slide 11: Make the ask.
Slide 12: List recognition options and prices for a gift at the level of the ask amount.
Slide 13: Summarize how the viewer can help meet the need.

trustees in a foundation meeting. If you have time to prepare for the meeting in advance, personalize the ask by creating an individual version of the PowerPoint presentation that makes a specific ask linked to a recognition opportunity for that one prospect.

Here are several ways to use a PowerPoint presentation in your campaign communications plan:

- Have it ready on a laptop with a screen in your on-site conference room and play it for all visitors.

- Burn the presentation onto a CD and include with all campaign packets.

- Show it on a big screen at events for prospects.

- Carry it with you on a laptop and use with individual prospects on a call.

- Put a copy up on your web site that can be downloaded for viewing.

E-newsletters, e-calendars, and e-blasts that include event information are also useful ways to use e-mail in campaign communication. E-newsletters are usually longer, newsy accounts of stories and facts related to the organization's work that are mailed electronically on a regular basis, often monthly or quarterly. These can contain information about upcoming events, but they are often used to feature photos and captions about events that have taken place, especially those that involve donor recognition.

E-calendars and e-blasts are shorter, more focused electronic messages that invite recipients to an event, announce an event, or provide a reminder before an event. All of these methods assume that you have a system for collecting the e-mail addresses of your supporters.

Find creative ways to collect e-mail addresses of prospects. For instance, offer a small gift or a break in the cost of one membership level for donors who sign up with their e-mail addresses. Most donors love small gifts, such as magnets, bumper stickers, and the like. You can use these items as incentives to gather e-mail addresses at events and community gatherings.

Proposal Writing for Results

The Expert's Mistake

A community center was preparing a proposal for a foundation to ask for funds to landscape its entire campus, a multiacre facility. It brought in an outside landscape expert to prepare a budget and write a report on what materials would be needed. Due to various delays, the budget and report were late and were rushed over to the nonprofit the day the proposal was due.

In a hurry to get the proposal out, the executive director bundled up the proposal, the budget, and the report and express mailed the package out immediately, without taking the time to read the report.

He was surprised when, three days later, the foundation director called him up to discuss the problems with the proposal. To his horror, he discovered upon reading the report that the expert had blamed the community center for a massive error in draining and site preparation when the original building was constructed. According to the expert, this error was the reason that all the previous landscaping had died, and, even worse, it would mean that the new plantings requested in the grant would suffer the same fate!

The executive director hastily withdrew the proposal, apologized to the foundation director, and called the expert. They discovered a misunderstanding regarding the site's drainage conditions that allowed the report to be redone in a more supportive fashion. The proposal was ultimately re-submitted and was successful in being funded.

Moral of the story: Read every page submitted with a grant proposal before it goes out.

Prepare and Test Strong Proposal Templates

If your campaign is lagging, it is important to review the actual written materials that your staff and volunteers are using to ask for funds. Preparing a strong proposal that is succinct, focused, compelling, and persuasive is harder than it sounds. Spend some time putting together a proposal template, one version for individual donors and a second version for foundations.

When you have a good draft in hand, try out the template on some willing testers, including a professional fundraising consultant. Your readers can help you find ways to sharpen your language, cut flowery descriptions, and shore up your case. Taking the time to write a good proposal is worthwhile, because the language can be used over and over again with different prospects throughout the remainder of the campaign.

Letters to Individual Prospects

For proposals that will be used with individual donors, consider a two- to three-page letter format. The letter does not have to cover every single detail about the campaign; it can be augmented with additional materials, such as the campaign brochure, budgets, the campaign PowerPoint copied onto a CD, or photos. Try to keep the materials organized in a folder or packet so that things don't fall out all over—you want your proposal to look clean, professional, and attractive.

Always use campaign stationery for the individual letter proposal. Campaign stationery should use the colors, design, and logo of the overall campaign. Consider printing the names of the campaign cochairs and campaign volunteers down one side of the campaign stationery (or across the bottom of the page). With these names in front of her, the prospect is being given a subtle message: Do not only read what we write here; look at all the people you know who already support this project.

The letter proposal should look clean and be easy to read. Proofread your drafts to make sure there are no small grammatical or spelling errors (donors tend to hold small mistakes against you when you are asking for money). Use wide margins, an 11 or 12 font size, and select a popular font that reads easily, such as Arial or Times Roman. Keep paragraphs all on the same page instead of breaking them at the bottom of a page—this helps to hold your themes together for the reader.

Break up the body of the letter proposal into sections with headings to convey key points quickly to the reader. The proposal should be able to be read in two different ways: The reader's eye should be able to scan the letter in about 20 seconds, read the headings, and glean the basic content; however, it should also deliver a strong punch if it is read in detail, word for word.

To break up the material, group two to three paragraphs under headings that are bolded and italicized, and skip a space between headings to separate each theme, topic, or set of ideas. Use headings to urge action or to highlight needs.

Just as when putting together a case statement, there are certain components that you should always include in a letter proposal. These include:

- A greeting and an explanation of the purpose of the letter.
- The name of the organization the proposal is coming from.
- The name of the individual being addressed for a gift.
- The amount of the ask (the dollar amount should be prominent in the letter, preferably in the first paragraph and repeated at least once elsewhere in the body of the letter).
- A brief summary of the mission and history of the organization.
- A brief summary of recent accomplishments of the organization.
- A statement of the need.
- The cost or budget for meeting the needs (a full budget can be referenced in the letter and included as an attachment).
- The ask spelled out (a description in words of how the recipient can help to meet the need through the proposed gift).
- The purpose and recognition for this specific ask amount.
- The reason why this need is urgent.
- Close with a summary of the ask, including the amount, the purpose and the timetable for the gift.

- The closing paragraph should include a next step, for instance: "We will call you next week to discuss this important project."
- Signatures should include those of the campaign chair (or the campaign volunteer assigned to this prospect) and the executive director/CEO.

It is usually not productive to send a letter proposal to an individual cold. The best use for a letter proposal is to mail it to the prospect after an individual call has been made. It thus serves as a summary of the call, the purpose, the need, the ask, and the recognition being offered. The prospect can use the letter to discuss the gift further with his wife, children, or accountant.

If it follows a personal call, the proposal can be personalized to include the specific gift amount and purpose that was discussed, and it should include answers to any questions that the prospect raised during the meeting. Be sure to reference a prior meeting in the first paragraph if one has taken place.

The proposal letter can also be used ahead of a personal call. This is one use where it is not absolutely necessary to include a dollar amount in the ask. The letter can make a strong case for support, but leave the ask amount for the personal face-to-face meeting. In this case, the letter could include a general appeal and end with a next step:

"Jenny, I will call you next week to set up an appointment to discuss your willingness to support this important need. We look forward to meeting with you soon."

Don't be afraid to tell a story in the individual proposal letter, but keep it short. The letter should not ramble on and on about who needs what. Using colorful language to evoke emotion can have its place, but do not take it too far and get maudlin or overly emotive. Do not make the proposal too formal or it will sound stilted. On the other hand, do not be too chummy, either. The letter proposal is a business proposition between the organization and the prospect, and it should use clean, clear, professionally appropriate prose.

Foundation Proposals that Make Your Case

Foundation proposals will contain some of the same elements that individual letter proposals contain, but they are often more formal and set out requirements for format, content, and delivery specifications.

Be sure first of all that your organization meets the requirements for applying to a specific foundation before writing the proposal. It is discouraging to do all the work of writing a proposal only to discover that the foundation does not fund capital projects, when that is what you were requesting funds for. Do your homework first! Look at the foundation's own web site to learn about application forms, previous gifts, deadlines, program interests, and requirements.

Foundations often specify a certain order for the content and copy by requiring that the proposal be submitted in an outline format. Make sure that you use the space provided to state all the important elements of your case, even if you add facts or elements that are not directly needed to respond to the questions asked.

Watching political debates can teach you how to provide answers to questions that say what you want them to say. You have probably noticed that most politicians do not always address the specific question they have been asked. They are trained to insert relevant information and new facts to support their approach to the issues in their responses, even if the response moves them slightly away from the original question. You can do this, too, but take care that you do provide an answer to the specific question before moving ahead to add ancillary information, or you will make the readers think you are avoiding the question.

Let us take an example. The proposal outline asks you to make a statement on the mission of your organization. State the mission in the first sentence, but immediately follow it with a second sentence (bolded below) that ties the mission to the need for more space (your case):

Our mission is to provide humane mental health care to all members of our community, regardless of income level. **In order to meet this mission, we must expand our** *facility to include more beds for more individuals who have lost their workplace-based health insurance due to job losses in the weakening economy.*

In another example, the foundation asks in the outline for you to identify your organization's community partnerships. Provide your answer with a brief list, but then tie the relationships back to the need for more space (your case):

We have partnerships across the community with both private and public mental health care providers; *however, due to the closing of a public community clinic in our region, the need for more beds has become acute.*

In other words, think first in overall terms about what you want the foundation trustees to learn about your organization and your case. Then work carefully within the guidelines you are given to include all of the major themes, facts, and arguments that you want to get across. Weave the story you want to tell into the structure of the application form that you are given. This can be a surprisingly creative enterprise! A good foundation proposal can be a masterpiece of persuasive prose posing in the structure of a dry outline.

The Personal Touch with Foundations

Proposals to foundations, like letter proposals to individuals, are often combined with an additional personal contact with a foundation trustee or program director. Don't be afraid to call the foundation. Many have program staff who are available to sound out interest areas and guide you on proposal requirements. Read the foundation web site, then call, and prepare your questions in advance. You want to sound smart and well-informed about their guidelines.

Some foundations encourage visits. Others prefer letters of inquiry. Call and ask if someone from the foundation is traveling to your region over the next few months. Follow the guidelines and develop as close a relationship as you can with an individual at the foundation office. If a foundation trustee or staff member will work with you, ask if she would be willing to review a draft of your proposal before you submit it.

Review lists of all foundation trustees with your campaign volunteers and board members before writing your proposal. If you discover a personal relationship, ask your volunteer to make a phone call to open the door for you or make a visit with the volunteer to the foundation office. Use whatever personal leverage you can to get the foundation to look in a friendly manner on your proposal. The very best writing in the world is not as impressive as having a foundation trustee meet with his old best friend, your campaign chair. Personal relationships can play an important role in foundation fundraising, just as they do with fundraising from individuals.

 IN THE REAL WORLD

After Hurricane Katrina, many generous donors were actively seeking ways they could contribute to the rebuilding of New Orleans. An administrator at one of the city's new public charter schools fielded a phone call from a woman who identified herself as a program officer at one of the country's largest and most recognizable national foundations.

"How can we help you?" the foundation caller asked (a question any fundraiser would die for).

"Well," said the administrator, "You have lots of money and we don't. Can't you just give us some?"

Needless to say, the foundation was not too impressed with this response. Although the foundation did eventually make a gift to the school, it required a coherent articulation of needs and the thoughtful pursuit of a project that would interest it to close the gift.

Using Online Applications and Cover Letters

Some foundations have recently begun to use rigidly constructed online applications for grants. The formats are often cumbersome and cannot be readily adjusted to use to make your case. Follow their directives, and then supplement the online application with a mailing that includes ancillary campaign materials and a personal cover letter. Unless the foundation specifically rules out additional proposal materials, it will probably add the new information to your file and use it in the decision making process. Also do not rule out making a personal call on these foundations. After all, just because they have an online process does not mean there are not humans back there reviewing everything.

Cover letters are an art form in themselves. Some foundations now explicitly reject cover letters and refuse to read them. Save your energy for those that might actually read the letter. The cover letter should be one page, addressed to a person, and signed by the CEO or campaign chair. If a volunteer knows a foundation trustee, ask that individual to sign the cover letter.

The cover letter should include a brief summary of the basic elements of the case—what the organization does, what you are asking for, why the project is needed, who will benefit—but use slightly different language from the proposal. Do not repeat exact sentences and phrases that the reader will encounter later in your materials.

Do not belabor points in the cover letter that are discussed in detail in the proposal. Use the cover letter to bring out a personal argument, such as why the volunteer signing the letter is involved with the organization. This gives the cover letter a unique twist (and human interest) that the proposal may lack.

Most foundations request a standardized package of attachments related to the governance and financial health of your organization. Review this information carefully before it is sent out. Requests for budgets, board lists, audits, and annual reports should be met, of course. But be aware of what these materials say about your organization and supply additional information to shore up any weaknesses.

If there has been an audit that is not completely clean, for instance, supply a follow-up letter from the auditor noting that the issues singled out have been taken care of. Do not leave a question in the mind of a foundation reader that could lead to doubt about your organization. Good financial health is a key ingredient of the review your proposal will receive from a foundation's board, and it needs to be clear that your financials are completely in order.

Good Communication about Bad Things

Now is a good time to have a crisis communication plan mapped out to help deal with unfortunate circumstances. In the case of major disruptions, such as hurricanes, fires, tornadoes, or acts of terrorism, the crisis plan may include moving the operation's core staff and services to a new site. Identify your emergency site ahead of the crisis and prepare staff and equipment to be transferred to that location.

Many organizations in post-Katrina New Orleans discovered too late after the flooding that they lost their databases. This can destroy operational and fundraising capability. To avoid this happening to you, designate an individual in each office or department who will be responsible for getting out that department's data. Store portable laptops on-site already loaded with the appropriate software, carry backup tapes, or contract with a server in another region of the country to maintain the database. Test everything to make sure it works before you need it.

It is also important to maintain communication with staff and board members during a crisis. In the case of Hurricane Katrina, for instance, New Orleans cell phones stopped working and only text messages could be sent and received for weeks following the storm. Consider requiring that all employees, parents, patients, and other constituents supply you with emergency out of town contact information in case it is needed. Designate a web site and/or emergency phone line that will be used for emergency information and updates. Use them frequently to keep your constituents informed.

It is also wise to address recent scandals, abrupt changes in leadership, the pending loss of accreditation, and other problems that may inconveniently raise their head directly with potential donors. It is better to address issues forthrightly and try to supply answers than to ignore them and risk looking like you hid damaging information.

If donors lose trust in your institution, it will hurt your relationship with them for a long time into the future, and they may even spread bad rumors about your organization to their colleagues. Honesty and trust are the watchwords of nonprofit funding relationships. If you lose your reputation, you have little left to bargain with.

IN THE REAL WORLD

A Loss of Trust

A college dean was meeting with a high level donor who was also an alumna and a member of the college's board; they met in the donor's penthouse apartment overlooking Central Park in New York City. The dean updated the donor on enrollment, finances, and programs, and then talked about the need for a new science building. They discussed the need and the plans for over an hour, then the dean left to catch a plane back to campus.

Two days later, the board member received a call from another alumnus seeking information about the bizarre accidental death of a student at the college that had taken place a week earlier. She was furious that the dean had not covered the situation with her during their meeting, and had, in fact, avoided any mention of it. In retrospect, the donor felt betrayed and was convinced the dean had not told her the truth about the incident because there was some cover-up going on. The relationship between the donor and the institution suffered for years because of this loss of trust.

KEY CONCEPT

Always tell your funders about negative things (scandals, the firing of the CEO, a bad audit, and so on) before they hear about it from someone else. You will increase their trust in your operation and also have the opportunity to tell them what happened on your own terms.

Summary

Improving communication with prospective donors is an important element of bringing your campaign back on track. First conduct an informal communications audit across your organization to see what messages are being communicated to donors from different departments. Then combine forces to create a powerful message from all across the institution, so that your case is being made from all sides.

Sharpen your case by targeting specific reasons for why a prospect should give and why making a gift is urgent. Use a variety of media, both print and electronic, to get your message across to potential donors. Making the case is not so much creating one definitive publication but rather identifying a clear message that everyone in the organization can use to support the campaign.

Proposal writing can also contain elements of the case. Learn how to use the application requirements for most foundations to make your case by answering questions with information you want the trustees to consider on your behalf. Also learn to write strong letter proposals for individual prospects in support of your case.

Strong communications programs require openness and honesty about the failings as well as the strengths of an organization. Do not hide bad news, but do find ways to get ahead of any crisis by telling your funders the news the way you want it to be expressed. Trust and good communications techniques go hand in hand.

CHAPTER 8

Build on Opportunities for Change across the Organization

After reading this chapter, you will be able to:

- Develop a viral Internet campaign to reach new audiences.
- Take advantage of new opportunities in a challenging environment.
- Reposition your organization through mergers and partnerships.

Change across the Organization

Change can be hard to manage. The current environment calls for enhanced flexibility and creative problem solving, but what does that mean in the context of a fundraising campaign? In this final chapter you will find several ideas for integrating change across your organization as well as in your advancement office.

The first section presents a case study that illustrates how to reach new audiences for a campaign by making use of the social networking properties of the Internet. In the second section, you will learn some tips for how to implement creative change in your fundraising programs. You will see how organizations can seize on new opportunities to become stronger, more flexible, and build donor loyalty.

Finally, we focus on how to use potential mergers and partnerships as a way to reposition your organization to meet new challenges. New partnerships can also open new doors for fundraising and donor support.

The Viral Internet Campaign

For some audiences, particularly younger donors, communicating through printed materials has gone out of fashion. We do not advise you to give up on print media completely, especially if your campaign relies on donors of age 55 and older. These are the donors who grew up with printed materials and are more comfortable seeing the facts written down in black and white. With donors in their teens, 20s and 30s, however, your organization may want to get in front of them with a focus on electronic messaging.

Case Study: The Louisiana SPCA

The Louisiana Society for the Prevention of Cruelty to Animals (LA/SPCA) provides a good example of the power of the Internet for creating an online giving community. The LA/SPCA has mounted an innovative Internet outreach effort to support the public phase of its $18 million capital campaign. Its campaign shows how a viral campaign can help you broaden your reach to new audiences and raise additional funds from new donors.

The purpose of the LA/SPCA campaign is to build a new shelter to replace its former facility, which was destroyed in the aftermath of Hurricane Katrina. The quiet phase of the campaign raised more than $10 million toward the $18 million goal, mostly from larger donors who were solicited personally by members of a campaign committee. The gifts given during the quiet phase ranged from $10,000 to a $2 million gift to name the new campus.

Giving during the public phase is divided into three different levels: major gifts of $10,000 and more are still being solicited by individuals; a new program to solicit gifts from $1,000 to $9,000 is under way; and gifts below $1,000 must be raised from a large number of donors.

As the group moved into planning for the public phase of the campaign, they began to think about ways to broaden their audience and build additional support from new donors at gift levels below $1,000. But how were new donors to be identified, cultivated, and solicited? Their answer was to mount an innovative viral Internet campaign.

The concept and the project were spearheaded by an LA/SPCA board member who is an executive at Peter Mayer Advertising, one of the oldest and best known PR firms in New Orleans.

What Is a Viral Campaign?

A viral campaign is an Internet-based fundraising initiative that creates an interactive online community where users can donate and share information about the cause they are supporting with others who share their interests. The team at Peter Mayer that created the viral campaign for the LA/SPCA defined its work from the beginning as not only creating an interactive site where the purpose was to give, but also to create a community where donors could share stories and photos of pets with people who had similar interests.

The Peter Mayer team comprised 10 professionals who each offered specific skills. This is not a project that your organization could take on without tapping into significant technical and creative expertise. If this expertise is available in-house, by all means use the skills available to you. For the LA/SPCA, the use of outside experts was a key requirement in getting the campaign up and running. The project group included the following staff members, who formed a creative team:

- Interactive creative director: conceptualized the project, kept it moving forward, identified appropriate links for social networking.
- Designer: created the look and feel of the site.
- Transactional strategist: focused on how to get the user to make a donation.

- Copy writer and producer: wrote the words on the site and created coordinated print ads.

- Project manager and account service rep: identified traditional media outlets, sold coordinated print ads.

- Developers (two): handled the technical side of creating the site and linked it to sites for social networking.

- Executive VP: managed the project, identified the team, and controlled costs.

The campaign site is available at **www.comestayheal.org/**. It is built around a very simple concept: people sharing photos and stories about happy dogs and cats. The message is intended to be uplifting, positive, and fun. This was planned to contrast with earlier post-Katrina themes used by the LA/SPCA in the silent phase of its campaign, which were focused on the devastation that the flooding in New Orleans wrought on the pet population. The creative team felt that three years past Katrina, with the flood receding in donors' minds, it was time to move on with an upbeat message.

The site architecture is designed to be simple and easy to navigate, and the design is open and friendly. It is meant to provide a contemporary update of the image of the LA/SPCA, which continues to have its own extensive organizational web site at **www.la-spca.org/**. Both sites use the same color palette, the same campaign logo, and develop similar themes. The two sites are linked through a banner on the home page of the original site, but they operate completely independently of each other.

On the home page of the campaign web site, each single donation fills in one square, contributing to an overall graphic element. The graphic fills up one square at a time as each gift is made, so the home page acts like a campaign thermometer that measures visually how many donations have been made. Running the cursor over each square in the graphic brings up a brief pet profile that has been posted by a donor.

Donors can upload photos and short stories about their pets after making their gift. Donors are encouraged to make more than one gift, because with each individual gift a new story and photo opportunity is available to them. This aspect gives users who have several pets the opportunity to display a square for each of their companion animals and keeps donors returning to use the site more than once.

To build out the site, additional pages are accessed from a short menu at the bottom of the home page. These additional pages use short blocks of text, accompanied by photos of pets, to explain the campaign, membership opportunities, frequently asked questions, and reasons to give. A special sculpture project encourages donors who give $125 or more to have their own personal inscription added to one of several silhouette animal sculptures to be displayed on the LA/SPCA campus.

The site is easy to navigate and is planned to motivate the user to make a transaction. The viewer is encouraged to stay on the site until a gift is made; thus, redirection to other sites is kept to a minimum. Every page contains the campaign logo with the campaign name: Come, Stay, Heal: Rebuilding the Louisiana SPCA.

Two buttons occupy a highly visible space in the top right-hand corner of every page, allowing the user to click to "Donate" or to "Share" the site with others. The buttons and the font size have been enlarged to accommodate readers of all ages, and the site navigation is very simple to avoid donor confusion.

Clicking on the Donate button brings the user to a page that offers giving levels ranging from $35 to $1,000. The site requires a $5 minimum gift, but in order to sight-raise with donors, larger gifts are encouraged through the display categories in the donate section. The gift level of $125 is prominently highlighted to attract donors through the use of a special recognition offer, inscribing the donor's name on an animal sculpture that will be erected on the SPCA campus.

While the pet stories and photos are available to all users, the ability to add their own story or to be recognized through a sculpture inscription is available to users only after a donation has been confirmed. Gifts are accepted through either a credit card or PayPal. The site architecture and layout are first focused on getting the user to give, then to encourage a higher level gift.

Links to Social Networking Sites

The user/viewer provides the viral aspect to the campaign. All donors are encouraged to share the campaign web site, and because they are sharing the story and photos of their own pets, they are more likely to share with their friends. Click on the Share button, and the site not only allows the user to e-mail the site's URL to a friend, but it offers several campaign logo "badges" featuring cute animals that can be placed on the user's personal web site. These badges create a link from the donor's personal site back to the campaign web site, so that the donor actually becomes a link in a network to share the site with other potential donors.

In addition to creating the web site for making gifts and sharing stories, the creative team developed online communities on several popular social networking sites to link people back to the campaign home page. These sites encourage a potential donor to move from a site that they are already using to the LA/SPCA campaign site. To select the best sites for its cause, the creative team developed a "lifestyle profile" of a potential donor. The team created links from sites and blogs that emphasize love of animals, fitness, and social causes, among other characteristics.

The social networking sites the team selected for linkage included Facebook, Dogster.com, and Catster.com. These sites are among a growing number of "pet destinations" on the Internet and were judged to attract viewers who might be attracted to give to the campaign based on the lifestyle profile.

 TIPS AND TECHNIQUES

Sharing Content on the Web

The LA/SPCA team worked to create links and comments about their campaign site on popular blogs and link aggregators such as Digg.com, Reddit.com, Delicious.com, StumbleUpon.com, and Twitter.com.

These are web sites made for people to discover and share content on the Internet and they provide a social bookmarking web service. They can

> influence the opinions of viewers and have the capacity to promote the viral aspect of the campaign by bringing the campaign web site to the attention of new audience members.

The way in which content is distributed on the Web has the potential to create a rapid chain of viewers for a site that is properly networked. Viewers who are interested will follow the links on these sites to the LA/SPCA site, thus developing an effective method of outreach to a new, broad audience of users who would never have encountered the LA/SPCA campaign through a more traditional format.

Campaign Rollout

Along with the online rollout of the campaign, which took advantage of the social networking capacity of the Internet to reach new viewers, the creative team also planned a more traditional rollout with a public event and an ad campaign in the print media to attract viewers to the site.

A holiday event for companion animals that has been part of the LA/SPCA's traditional Christmas party for local donors was reconfigured to serve as the kickoff of the new campaign web site. SPCA donors who attended the holiday party (along with their dogs) were each asked to provide a $10 contribution. All contributors were automatically enrolled in the new campaign and received access to their own square on the site home page. This allowed them to subsequently access the site in order to write their pet story and upload photos. The party included a huge outdoor screen where the new web site was prominently displayed, along with laptops showing the site on adjacent tables, so that all the attendees were made aware of the campaign.

In addition to the onsite promotion and linkages the team developed partnerships with traditional media outlets and other sponsors to help advertise the site. A 15-second video was created for YouTube and posted on local news sites. A print ad was featured in several New Orleans publications, including *Urban Dog*. The W Hotel, which has a pet-friendly guest policy, was tapped to host the kickoff event. All ad space was donated.

The campaign was built on the traditional PR concepts of maximizing the reach and the frequency of viewer impressions. With a mix of traditional and nontraditional media, the rollout was intended to increase both the number of times people saw a reference to the site and to broaden the demographic of the audience that was reached. The goal was to have the visual references and links to the site build on each other, so that the campaign would reach the largest number of potential supporters as many times as possible.

Could you create a viral campaign like this to accompany your own campaign web site? The sophistication and expertise provided by the Peter Mayer group was certainly a major component of the project's success. In this case, most of the work the creative team provided was done pro bono, but the actual cost of production and maintenance of a campaign along these lines could run from $75,000 to $100,000.

At the time of writing this book, it is too early to say how much money will be raised through the viral campaign. The goal for this portion of the public phase of the overall campaign is set at $500,000. With over 8,000 squares available for donors, the average gift would have to be $62 to meet the goal. The site has already received multiple small gifts from many donors, and the organization will attempt to convert these campaign donors into LA/SPCA members on an annual basis going forward.

This example of a viral campaign meets three different organizational goals: It provides donations for the public phase of a capital campaign; it promotes an online community of like-minded users that broadens the reach of the organization into new audiences; and it is a vehicle to attract users who can provide ongoing support for the organization beyond the campaign. A truly win-win effort for all concerned!

Lessons in Creative Problem-Solving

Given all the recent stresses experienced by our global economy, most nonprofits will have to think and act differently to survive the tough times. There are several concepts for dealing with long-term change that might help you and your organization emerge stronger while still sustaining or growing fundraising support.

KEY CONCEPT

Remain flexible and inspire the creativity of your staff and volunteers to help your organization face long-term challenges.

Those who worked with nonprofits in New Orleans directly following the destruction of Hurricane Katrina in 2005 had a crash course in creative problem solving. These examples come from the fundraising problems faced by many of the charter schools that were created in the city following the storm.

The charter schools were created in response to an unexpected opportunity following Katrina. The Orleans Parish School Board, which administered all the public schools in New Orleans, announced shortly after the hurricane that no public schools would be reopened in New Orleans for a full year.

In response, many parents, community organizers, and school administrators worked hard to turn their neighborhood public schools into charter schools. This gave them the option to reopen to meet demand as the population returned. As a result, by 2009 there were more than 50 public charter schools operating in New Orleans. The city is the first urban center where over 50 percent of the public school population attends a charter school.

The new charter schools faced huge obstacles when they reopened. They had to negotiate for space and buildings, manage site cleanup from hurricane damage, secure operational funding, create governing boards, provide services, find and hire teachers, and line up enrollment. Fundraising quickly became important to help meet some of these demands.

Several of the public schools that reorganized as charters raised more than $1 million each through private fundraising in the year following Katrina. These campaigns were quick, down and dirty. In each school, no prior fundraising infrastructure of any kind existed to build on. Prior to Katrina, these were public schools in a poor urban district with no staff or resources devoted to development.

How did these schools succeed in attracting so much financial support? Their methods included some novel ideas along with some new twists to generally accepted fundraising principles. Here are some of the more creative elements of their recovery campaigns along with the challenges they had to respond to:

1. *Problem: No mail was delivered in New Orleans for months following Katrina.* How to collect checks and money from donors for the schools?

   Solution: The high schools commandeered juniors and seniors to drive around the city picking up checks on call. Even young alumni were recruited when they returned home from college on vacations.

2. *Problem: The new schools needed to register as nonprofits and receive their status as a 501 (c) 3 in order to accept gifts.* The state took months to process these applications. How could the schools accept gifts before this status was approved?

   Solution: One school created a gift account with the New Orleans community foundation (the Greater New Orleans Foundation) to receive gifts, using the foundation's own nonprofit status.

3. *Problem: Lack of contact information for current students and families.* (More than half the population of New Orleans remained out of the city for at least one year following the flooding.)

   Solution: Student and parent groups set up e-mail and phone trees to track down and collect contact information for classmates. Web sites devoted to each school were key contact points for giving and receiving information and updates.

4. *Problem: No money to open school with.* (Federal, state, and city funds were allocated to charters based on enrollments months after the schools opened.)

Solution: One of the charters asked for and received a large loan from a local foundation that wanted to see the schools open. The loan was paid back from private grants and public funds received later in the year.

5. *Problem: No fiscal track record for donors to rely on.*

   Solution: The new charters were required to create independent governing boards. They selected board members who were experienced in financial matters and trusted throughout the community. Funders relied on the boards to oversee finances during the first year of operation, and then audits were conducted and provided to funders.

These schools have rebounded, and to their credit, are producing better educated students with better test scores than the system produced before the storm. One of the most significant qualities that this array of new charter schools has exhibited is flexibility in problem solving—across the board, not just in fundraising. If they could find creative solutions to problems in post-Katrina New Orleans without mail delivery or start-up funds, you can do it in your organization with all the assets you have to draw upon.

Diversify Sources of Funding

One of the main strategies recommended in this book has been to diversify sources of funding. Identifying new prospects, developing new outreach programs through the Internet, and seeking a balance between individual, corporate, and foundation giving sources all have the same concept in common: Diversify risk by seeking funding from a variety of sources.

 IN THE REAL WORLD

The Madoff Scandal Rocked the Foundation World

"Bernard L. Madoff is the investor accused in a major Ponzi scheme that continues to reverberate through the business and charity worlds," *The*

(Continued)

Chronicle of Philanthropy wrote on December 22, 2008, in an article entitled, "Charities Reel from Investor Scandal."

The Madoff scandal, with an alleged loss of over $50 billion to investors, has destroyed major Jewish family foundations across the country, including The Picower Foundation, in Palm Beach, Fla., with assets of $1 billion. Others that got caught up in the investment scam include the Elie Wiesel Foundation for Humanity, Yeshiva University, and Steven Spielberg's Wunderkinder Foundation, according to the *Wall Street Journal* on December 23, 2008.

The main problem that led to the downfall of these philanthropic organizations was putting their trust—and their money—in one person's investment scheme. That person appears to be a crook, and their assets went down with him. The lesson to learn from this tragedy is to diversify sources of funding. Those nonprofits that depended heavily on one foundation or one donor who was affected were the first to fail. Also be sure that your institution's endowment has a diversified investment policy. Do not put all your eggs in one basket! Donors are now asking tough questions about investment policies to be sure that their gifts are invested wisely.

The concept of diversification can also be useful when looking at fundraising programs. Focus on three programs: one that will help your organization bring in cash right away, one program to support major needs, and one long-term program to provide support into future years. These might include the annual fund, the campaign (or portions of a revised campaign), and a planned giving program. Each of these programs attracts a different kind of donor. You will be capable of attracting a diverse array of donors by running effective programs in these three areas.

Another area where diversification is important is in finding sources of financial support beyond private philanthropy. While certain portions of state and local funding may become tighter in a struggling economy, there will most likely be major changes at the federal level with the new administration arriving in Washington.

Look for federal funds designated to support economic stimulation and job growth that may give your organization new ways to work with new audiences. Consider ways to revise the services offered by your organization (still focused on your mission, of course) to meet newly defined funding priorities.

Also encourage your staff and volunteers to think of ways to increase income from revenue-producing programs. Perhaps your group should think about renting out unused space, charging for special services offered, or producing a new item for sale online. Be creative about ways to make money and reduce your reliance on charitable giving.

Finally, diversification can also be helpful as a concept in messaging. While your communication strategist will want to focus on the creation of a few key messages, think about adding some new venues for getting your message to the public. Here are some ways to diversify your communication strategies:

- Ask to use free billboards (advertising is down nationally).

- Create an online community and develop ways for your donors to interact with your organization and each other by exchanging stories, ideas, blogs, and photos online.

- Hold a contest for the best logo, theme, photo, or story related to your mission.

- Develop a strong PowerPoint presentation as a template, and then individualize it for each call on a major donor.

- Develop a new message based on why a donor should give now, more than ever, to meet the needs your organization serves in the community.

Be sure to coordinate your messaging strategy across the entire organization, so that you do not find one side of the institution presenting a message or theme that is completely different from the case for fundraising.

Seize Opportunities to Create Positive Change

Recessions do not last forever, and the global economy will most likely bounce back somewhere down the road. If you have positioned your programs and your organization to take advantage of new opportunities as they arise, you will emerge stronger and better equipped to face both good times and bad.

Opportunities in Staffing

The mass layoffs hitting industry may actually end up benefitting the not-for-profit labor pool. A large number of attractive, high-performing white-collar workers are looking for stable and rewarding jobs. The nonprofit community may be the right place for many of them to land. How can you tell if someone making the switch from a for-profit sector job (such as banking or investment planning) would make a good employee?

Use the quiz in Exhibit 8.1 to rate your potential employees from the for-profit sector.

EXHIBIT 8.1

Quiz for Prior For-Profit Employees Applying for a Fundraising Position in the Nonprofit Sector

(Score one point for each "yes" answer and zero points for each "no" answer. See scoring table on the following page.)

1. *Does the candidate understand and wholeheartedly support the mission of your organization?*

2. *Does the candidate have strong skills in communication areas, especially in writing and speaking?*

3. *Can the candidate work for a lower salary than he was making in his former position without becoming resentful?*

4. *Has the candidate had any volunteer experiences among her past activities?*

5. *Does the candidate bring with him substantive connections with new potential individuals or groups of supporters?*

6. *Does the candidate seem upbeat, positive, and energetic?*

7. *Is the candidate ready to make a long-term commitment to this career switch?*

8. *Is there evidence that the candidate's family/spouse/significant other will also support this career switch?*

9. *Is the candidate being completely honest and above-board with you?*

10. *Does the candidate have the ability to grow with your organization and contribute more over the long term?*

Key:

For a score of 8 to 10: Hire that person today!

For a score of 5 to 7: Make sure someone else interviews the candidate, and get a second opinion.

For a score below 5: Tell the candidate to go back to banking.

At several points in this book we have argued against cutting advancement staff in the midst of economic turmoil in order to keep the fundraising engine chugging. You may be able to find good arguments to hire additional staff, or to replace a position that has been downsized, with skilled employees laid off from other jobs.

If you can identify and hire a highly skilled employee who has been laid off from the for-profit sector, and who fits well with your organization, take this opportunity to do so. Make sure to discuss salaries, benefits, future raises, and opportunities for professional advancement carefully with these job candidates, as their job satisfaction is the key to their success with you.

Here are some professional sectors where employees' skills may transfer well into the nonprofit fundraising arena:

- Stock brokers: used to making cold calls, understand how to talk about money, and usually can explain tax-wise giving (gifts using planned giving tools).

- Bankers: often know where the wealth is buried, can talk about money, are used to handling confidential financial transactions.

- Public relations executives: can sell services, know how to please clients, are professional in their approach to meeting the clients' needs.

- Teachers: have patience with explaining things to donors; know how to engage and keep the donor's interest; often have strong communications skills.

- Sales professionals: know how to cultivate and ask, not afraid to close a gift, but could be too pushy for development work, depending on their personality.

When hiring employees who have never worked in the nonprofit world before, *fit* becomes an important factor. Look carefully at personal indications of temperament and style, and check to see that the individual is comfortable with different types of personalities when you conduct interviews. The personal qualities you will find most attractive over the long term include a strong work ethic, giving good value for the time at work, honesty, compassion, and directness. A dose of humility does not hurt, either!

IN THE REAL WORLD

At one university, candidates for the VP for advancement position were required to interview with at least 10 different groups on campus. One of the meetings was set up in the student center with a selected group of student leaders. These student leaders worked with the advancement office doing various outreach and fundraising projects across the community, so their input into the search was considered valuable.

One candidate was accidentally misdirected to the wrong room, where she waited impatiently for students who never appeared. She stormed out after waiting for 15 minutes and complained loudly to the administrative staff that she was "tired of people wasting her time."

Upon hearing this report, the search committee declared that the candidate had shown her true colors, and they all voted against her candidacy. They were so taken with the subtle method they had created accidentally to test a candidate's temperament that they faked the misstep and sent all their other candidates to the wrong room, too.

Opportunities to Engage Your Supporters

Nonprofits have long been aware that their supporters tend to be engaged in activities related to their mission. We have discussed some ways to analyze donor engagement in Chapter 2 by measuring the volunteer activity levels of donors to your organization. Now the options for engagement have expanded even further due to the economic downturn.

Volunteers have always been a wonderful source of aid to nonprofits, and many nonprofits could not operate at all without their volunteer cadre of support. If your organization is experiencing downsizing, consider how to get more work accomplished by volunteers. They are not only a great source of help; they can attract friends and colleagues to your cause.

Ask your donors, on a selective basis, to become involved in a meaningful way in the work of your organization (see Exhibit 8.2 for ideas on how to do

---

EXHIBIT 8.2

Areas Where Donors Can Be Asked to Donate Time and Skills in Addition to Their Money

- Ask CPAs and attorneys to sit on a planned giving committee. They should not be asked to provide direct financial advice to donors, but they can help you with policy, marketing, and recognition related to planned gifts.

- Ask PR executives to assist with ad campaigns, logos, graphic design, marketing materials, and other communication outreach efforts.

- Ask donors who also give to political campaigns or who have political ties in your community to introduce you to key policy makers at the local, state, and national levels.

- Ask donors to bring a friend to a cultivation event.

- Ask donors to travel with you to events or meetings with out-of-town prospects to share their enthusiasm for your organization.

- In a university or school setting, ask donors to provide internships, to mentor young people, and to help them network to find jobs after they graduate.

- For donors in corporate settings, ask them to help you organize a volunteer day in which a group of their employees take a service day to work

(Continued)

with your organization. Ideas could include tutoring, landscaping, speaking at career days, or providing field trips to the corporate site.

- Engage donors through social networking via the Internet. Create an interactive web site that allows supporters to post comments, share stories, upload photos, and remain in communication with each other through the organization.

this). It will help to cultivate their engagement, increase their understanding of your mission, and alleviate staffing shortfalls.

Donors who donate money, time, and skills are more likely to remain committed to your organization over the long run than people who just write a check. Find ways to keep your donors involved and you will also help the bottom line.

Repositioning in Tough Times

Not all nonprofits will make it through these tough times. Be prepared to take advantage of opportunities that require major strategic and structural changes in your organization. Having the vision to bring together new partnerships could assure that your organization will emerge stronger and more able to serve your community from these challenges.

Assess the Landscape for New Partners

Look for mergers, acquisitions, and partnerships that give your organization a strategic advantage in the nonprofit marketplace. In the for-profit world, the current economic challenges are creating winners and losers. Think about how to make your organization a winner in the increasingly competitive environment for nonprofit dollars. One of those methods is to create new partnerships that help to break down old barriers.

When looking for groups to merge or partner with, start with mission. You will be able to work better through the inevitable difficulties that will arise in a merger or partnership if the missions of the two organizations are at least aligned. Style differences can cause trouble, but mission differences can cause a divorce.

Look for partners that will bring you a competitive advantage. If your constituents are mostly 50 years in age plus, look for an organization that can bring you young supporters. If the audience your organization serves is mostly white and middle-aged, consider a partnership with a nonprofit that serves a minority population. The new partnership should allow you to tap different sectors of support, apply to new foundations, create new funding opportunities, and develop new programs. It should create value, not just spread the risk.

Looking for new partners will give you a much-needed shot in the arm toward repositioning your organization and your fundraising efforts. Here are some ways to explore new partnerships:

- Provide space for another nonprofit that is outgrowing its site. Take advantage of the presence of their programs on your site to package both organizations' services together in a manner that builds on each group's strong points.

- Develop a program with a nonprofit that serves a completely different audience from yours. Find a foundation that supports joint efforts and apply for a grant that will pay for the partnership programs.

- Try advertising your nonprofit services jointly with another organization that has a complementary mission. Save on costs while creating a distinct identity for each group.

- Develop one component of your fundraising plan together with another organization. Share mailing lists or prepare a combined call on several key prospects. Use the strengths of both organizations to open the door to a donor whom you have not been able to reach all by yourself.

- Offer to provide expertise to another nonprofit for a program area where they are weak and you are strong. Develop the partnership by soliciting support for the new program and combine fundraising efforts.

- Use partnerships to improve your record of community outreach and service by working with smaller, less well-established groups, including those that serve minority and underserved populations. Write stories about these partnerships for your publications, web sites, proposals, and other communication efforts. Show donors that your organization practices what it preaches.

IN THE REAL WORLD

A Partnership in Art

A prominent urban art museum was asked to offer public exhibition space for the display of a valuable collection of African American art that belonged to a small, regional research center and library.

The museum entered into the partnership with the twin goals of reaching new audiences and expanding its educational outreach into the African American community. The research center was eager to partner with a prominent art museum that could provide space and visibility in an appropriate venue for the exhibition. Both sides were happy to meet their goals through the initial plan for the exhibition.

As curators, board members, and executive directors of the two organizations started working together, a new synergy began to develop. The partnership expanded on some levels that had not been anticipated in the original discussions. The initial step was taken when each board asked the executive director of the other organization to serve on its board. This was followed by a broad mandate to develop educational programs and outreach into the community in the name of both organizations working together.

Ultimately the two institutions developed a grant proposal together and submitted it to a national foundation that supports the arts on behalf of the new partnership. Both institutions received financial support for their joint programs as a result of the grant begin funded. The partnership ended up affecting not only the exhibition schedule, but also board membership, program offerings, and fundraising opportunities at both institutions.

Summary

There are numerous ways to nurse a failing fundraising campaign back to good health. Some campaigns will require changes in strategy and structure of key elements like goals, recognition, and timetables. Other campaigns will benefit from reaching out to new audiences with new communication efforts, such as the viral Internet campaign described in this chapter.

You and your colleagues will also want to take a broader look at how to take advantage of opportunities that arise due to the tough economic environment. Use the challenges your organization faces to unleash the creative ideas of staff and volunteers. Find ways to ask volunteers to do more so that they become truly engaged in the work of your organization. If you can find the means in your budget, hire new staff from the legion of bankers, stock brokers, and other white-collar professionals who are being laid off.

There may come a time when your organization desires to change its structure through a merger or new partnerships. Look for nonprofit partners that have a mission that dovetails well with your own. Find synergies in fundraising and program development with former competitors. Take charge of your own fate, and that of your organization, by managing the change around you, being decisive and providing good leadership.

Good luck and good fundraising!

Index